MUSIC ★ ICONS

MARLEY

LUKE CRAMPTON & DAFYDD REES
WITH WELLESLEY MARSH

TASCHEN

HONG KONG   KÖLN   LONDON   LOS ANGELES   MADRID   PARIS   TOKYO

CONTENTS

1

BOB MARLEY
JAMMIN'

JAMMIN'

JAMMIN'

BOB MARLEY: JAMMIN'

Only a handful of artists can lay claim to popularizing an entire music genre: singer-songwriter/guitarist Bob Marley is one. His name is synonymous with the indigenous Jamaican offbeat music of reggae, a local genre he took from his beloved island homeland to the world. The first reggae superstar, the dreadlocked, ganja-smoking Marley became a musical ambassador not only for the rhythmic Caribbean music that he helped create, but also for themes of peace, revolution, poverty, spirituality, love, and the Rastafarian philosophy.

Marley (b. Nesta Robert Marley, February 6, 1945, Nine Miles, St. Ann Parish, Jamaica), left school at the age of 14 with a notable interest in playing music with his childhood friend Bunny Livingston and musicians Peter Tosh and Junior Braithwaite—often under the tutelage of Joe Higgs,—a Kingston-based pioneer of the "ghetto music" that was percolating in the Trench Town slums. For the young street rebels struggling with the hardships of Trench Town life, music and soccer were the best diversions.

After being brought to the attention of Kingston record-label owner and producer Leslie Kong, Marley recorded the self-penned *Judge Not* for Kong's Beverley's label in 1962, followed by *One Cup Of Coffee*. The Wailers formed in 1964 with core musicians Livingston (soon known as Bunny Wailer), Braithwaite (who exiled to the United States in 1964), and Tosh, and the group began a short though prolific recording relationship with another top Kingston producer, Clement Seymour "Sir Coxsone" Dodd, owner of the Studio One label.

Initially playing a local rhythmic brew of American-influenced R & B, rocksteady, and "Rude Boy" ska, The Wailers began honing a tighter form of pure reggae, augmented by female backing singers Beverly Kelso, Cherry Green, and Alpharita Anderson (aka Rita), whom Marley married in February 1966. The same year he took an eight-month trip to be with his relocated mother in Wilmington, Delaware, United States, and returned to Kingston where The Wailers had fully adopted the Rastafarian faith that would direct their spiritual lives and much of their music.

Having built an increasingly loyal following in Jamaica, but having received minimal financial reward to date, 1970 saw the release of **The Best Of The Wailers**, regarded by many as the first truly commercial reggae album, a set which reunited Marley and The Wailers with producer Kong. They subsequently recorded some four dozen seminal reggae gems (including *Soul Rebel, No Sympathy*, and *African Herbsman*) together with burgeoning Jamaican producer Lee "Scratch" Perry. Perry sold the masters to British reggae specialist label, Trojan Records, allegedly withholding the 50 percent advance due to the band. Once again feeling burned by the deal, the group established its own label, Tuff Gong (Marley's nickname).

With Marley having spent much of the year in England with Johnny Nash, in 1972 he and The Wailers signed to Island Records, a successful UK indie owned by Jamaican entrepreneur/producer Chris Blackwell. With Marley depicted on its front cover smoking a huge spliff, **Catch A Fire** featured eight (of nine) cuts written by him (including one cowritten with Tosh). This extraordinary mainstream debut finally introduced his unique music, image, and talent to an international audience. With social themes of oppression and emancipation, this album and its follow-up, **Burnin'**, set the defiant tone for much of Marley's subsequent work—though it was the last to feature his long-standing musical compadres and equal partners, Bunny Wailer and Peter Tosh. Thereafter, and now billed as Bob Marley and The Wailers, Marley was essentially a solo artist and increasingly regarded as the principal architect and messenger of the reggae genre. With worldwide acclaim increasing with each album and tour, Marley also became instrumental in spreading the word of his devout Rastafarian faith—and its dreadlocked style and culture—musically culminating in his final studio release, **Uprising**, in 1980.

Among many cover versions of Marley's iconic songs, Eric Clapton's 1974 reworking of *I Shot The Sheriff*—originally featured on **Burnin'**—gave Marley his first global success as a writer. Curiously, Marley's biggest hit and signature song was one of the few not officially credited to him: His live version of *No Woman, No Cry* was credited to Vincent Ford, an old friend of Marley's who managed a soup kitchen in Trench Town, though Marley subsequently mentioned, in a 1975 JA TV interview, that he wrote the song himself on Ford's guitar.

With his life cruelly cut short by cancer at only 36, Marley's entire recording career spanned only 19 years—during which time he created a canon of work that is more popular today than at any other time. His greatest-hits collection, **Legend**, remains, by far, the best-selling reggae album of all time, while his 1977 opus, **Exodus**, was named Album of the Century by **Time** magazine in 1999. Posthumously inducted into the Rock and Roll Hall of Fame in 1994 and honored with the Grammy Lifetime Achievement Award in 2001, Marley's music, image, and spirit have transcended his own mortality.

BOB MARLEY: JAMMIN'

Es gibt nur eine Handvoll Musiker auf der Welt, die von sich behaupten können, eine ganze Stilrichtung populär gemacht zu haben: Bob Marley, Sänger, Komponist und Gitarrist, ist einer von ihnen. Sein Name steht für den aus Jamaika stammenden Reggae mit seinem charakteristischen Offbeat. Bob Marley brachte ihn von seiner geliebten Heimatinsel mit und trug ihn hinaus in die Welt. Er war der erste Reggae-Superstar und wurde, Gras rauchend und mit seinen Dreadlocks, zum musikalischen Botschafter der rhythmischen Musik der Karibik und darüber hinaus zum Botschafter für Themen wie Frieden, Revolution, Armut, Spiritualität, Liebe und Rastafari-Bewegung.

Marley wurde am 6. Februar 1945 als Nesta Robert Marley in Nine Miles, St. Ann Parish auf Jamaika geboren. Im Alter von 14 Jahren verließ er die Schule und fing an zusammen mit seinem Freund aus Kindertagen Bunny Livingston und den Musikern Peter Tosh und Junior Braithwaite zu musizieren – oft unter Anleitung von Joe Higgs, einem Pionier der „Ghetto Music", die damals im Slumviertel Trench Town in Kingston kursierte. Für die Straßenjungen, die in Trench Town ums Überleben kämpften, waren Musik und Fußball die einzigen Möglichkeiten, der harten Realität des Lebens im Slum zu entfliehen.

Leslie Kong, Produzent und Inhaber eines Plattenlabels in Kingston, wurde auf Marley aufmerksam und ließ ihn 1962 für sein Label Beverley's seine Eigenkomposition *Judge Not* aufnehmen, die nächste Einspielung war *One Cup Of Coffee*. 1964 wurde die Band The Wailers gegründet, zu deren hartem Kern Livingston (bald als Bunny Wailer bekannt), Braithwaite (der 1964 in die USA auswanderte) und Tosh gehörten. Die junge Band begann eine kurze, aber produktive Zusammenarbeit mit einem weiteren wichtigen Produzenten in Kingston, mit Clement Seymour „Sir Coxsone" Dodd, dem Besitzer des Labels Studio One.

The Wailers spielten anfangs ein lokal eingefärbtes, rhythmisches Gemisch aus amerikanisch beeinflusstem R 'n' B, Rocksteady und „Rude Boy" Ska. Bald begannen sie an einer reineren Form des Reggae zu arbeiten, unterstützt von den Backgroundsängerinnen Beverly Kelso, Cherry Green und Alpharita Anderson (Rita), die Marley im Februar 1966 heiratete. Im selben Jahr ging Marley nach Wilmington, Delaware, in den USA, wohin seine Mutter ausgewandert war, er kehrte aber nach acht Monaten zurück nach Kingston. The Wailers hatten mittlerweile den Rastafari-Glauben angenommen, der Leben und Musik von nun an spirituell prägte.

Bob Marley and The Wailers hatten sich zwar eine treue Anhängerschaft in Jamaika aufgebaut, aber finanziell bisher kaum von ihren Schallplattenaufnahmen profitiert. 1970 kam **The Best Of The Wailers** heraus. Die Platte galt weithin als erstes kommerzielles Reggae-Album und brachte Marley und The Wailers wieder mit Produzent Kong zusammen. Anschließend nahmen sie an die fünfzig große Reggae-Hits auf (darunter *Soul Rebel*, *No Sympathy* und *African Herbsman*) und arbeiteten mit dem erfolgreichen jamaikanischen Produzenten Lee „Scratch" Perry zusammen. Perry verkaufte die Masterbänder an das britische, auf Reggae spezialisierte Label Trojan Records, wobei er den Bandmitgliedern den ihnen zustehenden fünfzigprozentigen Vorschuss angeblich vorenthielt. Die Gruppe fühlte sich von Neuem hintergangen und gründete ihr eigenes Label Tuff Gong (Marleys Spitzname).

Marley hatte einen Großteil des Jahres 1972 mit Johnny Nash in England verbracht und wurde mit The Wailers bei Island Records, einem erfolgreichen englischen Indie-Label, das dem jamaikanischen Unternehmer und Produzenten Chris Blackwell gehörte, unter Vertrag genommen. Die LP **Catch A Fire** zeigte auf dem Cover Marley mit einem Riesenjoint; acht der neun Titel hatte er selbst geschrieben, einen zusammen mit Tosh. Durch dieses bemerkenswerte Mainstreamdebüt wurde Marleys einzigartige Musik, Begabung und Lebensphilosophie endlich einem internationalen Publikum bekannt. Mit gesellschaftlich relevanten Themen wie Unterdrückung und Gleichberechtigung gab dieses Album zusammen mit dem Nachfolgealbum **Burnin'** den rebellischen Ton für Marleys spätere Arbeit an – es war allerdings die letzte Zusammenarbeit mit seinen langjährigen musikalischen Kompagnons und gleichberechtigten Partnern Bunny Wailer und Peter Tosh. Danach nannte er sich zwar Bob Marley and The Wailers, war von nun an aber im Grunde ein Solomusiker und wurde als der eigentliche Begründer und Botschafter der Reggaemusik angesehen. Sein Ruhm wurde mit jeder Platte und Tournee größer, was Marley dazu benutzte, den Rastafari-Glauben auf der Welt bekannt zu machen – zusammen mit dem Dreadlockstil und der damit verbundenen Lebensweise. Seinen musikalischen Höhepunkt erreichte er mit der letzten Studioeinspielung **Uprising** 1980.

Neben vielen anderen Coverversionen von Marleys legendären Stücken bescherte Eric Claptons Fassung des Songs *I Shot The Sheriff* von 1974 – ursprünglich war der Song auf dem Album **Burnin'** herausgekommen – Marley den ersten weltweiten Erfolg als Songwriter. Seltsamerweise stammt Marleys größter Hit, mit dem er am stärksten identifiziert wird, als einer der wenigen zumindest offiziell nicht von ihm selbst: Seine Live-Version von *No Woman, No Cry* wird Vincent Ford zugeschrieben, der ein alter Freund von Marley war und eine Suppenküche in Trench Town führte. Marley erwähnte später in einem Interview von 1975 mit dem Fernsehsender JA TV, er habe den Song selbst komponiert, allerdings auf Fords Gitarre.

Bob Marleys Leben fand viel zu früh durch Krebs ein Ende, als er erst 36 Jahre alt war. Seine gesamte Karriere von der ersten bis zur letzten Plattenaufnahme währte nur 19 Jahre – doch in dieser Zeit schuf er ein Werk, das heute populärer ist als je zuvor. Seine Greatest-Hits-Collection **Legend** ist nach wie vor das bestverkaufte Reggae-Album aller Zeiten und seine LP **Exodus** (1977) wurde vom **Time** magazine 1999 zum Album des Jahrhunderts erklärt. Posthum wurde er 1994 in die Rock and Roll Hall of Fame aufgenommen und 2001 mit dem Grammy Lifetime Achievement Award für sein Lebenswerk geehrt. Marleys Musik und sein Lebensstil wirken weit über seinen Tod hinaus.

BOB MARLEY : JAMMIN'

Rares sont les artistes ayant réussi le tour de force d'incarner et de populariser à eux seuls tout un genre musical : l'auteur-compositeur-interprète et guitariste Bob Marley est de ceux-là. Son nom est synonyme de la musique chaloupée des autochtones de la Jamaïque, un genre local né sur sa chère terre insulaire et exporté par l'artiste aux quatre coins du monde. La première superstar du reggae, l'homme aux dreadlocks, fumeur de *ganja*, est devenu l'ambassadeur de cette musique caribéenne qu'il a contribué à créer, mais aussi de la paix, de la révolution, de la cause des déshérités, de la spiritualité, de l'amour et de la philosophie rastafari.

Bob Marley, de son vrai nom Nesta Robert Marley, naît le 6 février 1945 à Rhoden Hall, un hameau de la paroisse de Saint Ann situé près de Nine Miles, sur l'île de la Jamaïque. Marley quitte l'école à l'âge de 14 ans. Il aime passer son temps à faire de la musique avec son ami d'enfance Bunny Livingston, Peter Tosh et Junior Braithwaite – souvent sous la houlette bienveillante de Joe Higgs, pionnier de la « musique du ghetto » à Kingston, qui ratissait les taudis de Trench Town à la recherche de nouveaux talents. (Pour ces jeunes rebelles issus de la rue, qui luttent jour après jour contre les épreuves de la vie à Trench Town, la musique et le football sont les meilleurs moyens d'évasion.)

En 1962, à Kingston, Marley attire l'attention du producteur Leslie Kong et enregistre pour sa maison de disques, Beverley's, le titre *Judge Not*, de sa propre composition. Il le signe Robert Marley. Pour son prochain titre, *One Cup Of Coffee*, il choisit le nom de Bobby Martell. Les Wailers se forment en 1964 autour du noyau dur constitué de Livingston (bientôt rebaptisé Bunny Wailer), Braithwaite (qui s'exile aux États-Unis la même année) et Tosh ; le groupe entame alors une collaboration courte mais prolifique avec un autre important producteur de Kingston, Clement Seymour « Sir Coxsone » Dodd, patron du label Studio One.

Les Wailers, qui jouent au départ un mélange local de R & B d'inspiration américaine, de rocksteady, de ska « Rude Boy » et d'accompagnements traditionnels, fournissent en studio un reggae plus resserré, plus pur, enrichi par les voix féminines de Beverly Kelso, Cherry Green et Alpharita Anderson (Rita), que Marley épouse en février 1966. La même année, il rend une visite de huit mois à sa mère, installée aux États-Unis, à Wilmington (Delaware), puis retourne à Kingston où les Wailers se sont convertis à la foi rastafari ; elle guidera leurs vies spirituelles et inspirera une grande partie de leur musique.

Le groupe séduit un public de plus en plus vaste en Jamaïque, mais tire peu de bénéfices de ses nombreux enregistrements ; en 1970 sort la compilation **The Best Of The Wailers**. Généralement considéré comme le premier album de reggae commercial, il marque les retrouvailles entre Marley (et les Wailers) et Kong. Ils enregistrent plus tard une quarantaine de perles du reggae – parmi lesquelles *Soul Rebel*, *No Sympathy* et *African Herbsman* – avec le producteur jamaïcain en pleine ascension Lee «Scratch» Perry. Après avoir vendu les bandes au label britannique Trojan Records, qui s'est spécialisé dans le reggae, Perry est accusé d'avoir gardé pour lui les 50 pour cent d'avance destinés aux musiciens. Le groupe, se sentant une fois de plus floué, crée un nouveau label indépendant, Tuff Gong (le surnom de Marley).

Bob Marley passe la majeure partie de l'année 1972 en Angleterre avec Johnny Nash ; avec les Wailers, il signe un contrat avec Island Records, un prospère label indépendant britannique appartenant à l'entrepreneur et producteur jamaïcain Chris Blackwell. Huit des neuf titres de **Catch A Fire**, dont la pochette montre Marley en train de fumer un énorme joint, ont été écrits et composés par Marley, qui cosigne le neuvième avec Tosh. Avec cette extraordinaire plongée dans le *mainstream*, un public international découvre sa musique, son image et son talent exceptionnels. Cet album – tout comme le suivant, **Burnin'** – aborde des problèmes de société tels que l'oppression et l'émancipation : il donne le ton – rebelle, provocateur – de l'œuvre ultérieure de Marley, même si ses camarades et partenaires de toujours, Bunny Wailer et Peter Tosh, signent là leur dernière collaboration. Lorsqu'ils quittent le groupe, Marley prend réellement une stature d'artiste solo, accompagné par les Wailers, et devient le principal architecte et messager du reggae. Ses admirateurs sont plus nombreux à chaque sortie d'album et à chaque tournée, et Marley profite de cette renommée pour répandre la bonne parole du mouvement rastafari, ainsi que sa culture et son style, jusqu'à atteindre son apogée musical dans son dernier album studio, **Uprising**, en 1980.

Parmi les nombreuses reprises des plus célèbres chansons de Marley, la version de *I Shot The Sheriff* (titre de l'album **Burnin'**) remaniée par Eric Clapton en 1974 offre à Marley son premier succès mondial en tant que compositeur. Curieusement, le titre sans doute le plus célèbre de Marley n'est pas officiellement signé de sa main : sa version live de *No Woman, No Cry* est en effet attribuée à Vincent Ford, un vieil ami de Marley qui gérait une soupe populaire à Trench Town – même si Marley affirmera, lors d'une interview donnée en 1975 à JA TV, avoir composé lui-même la chanson sur la guitare de Ford.

Emporté prématurément par un cancer à l'âge 36 ans, sa carrière musicale n'aura duré que 19 ans ; dix-neuf années au cours desquelles il a donné corps à une œuvre plus populaire aujourd'hui que jamais. La compilation de ses plus grands succès, **Legend**, demeure, et de loin, l'album de reggae le plus vendu dans le monde, et son opus de 1977, **Exodus**, a été élu Album du siècle par le **Time** magazine en 1999. Honoré à titre posthume par une entrée au Rock and Roll Hall of Fame en 1994 et par le Grammy Lifetime Achievement Award en 2001, Marley nous a légué une musique, une iconographie et une âme qui ont transcendé sa condition de mortel.

2

CHRONOLOGY

CHRONOLOGIE

CHRONOLOGIE

THE 1960^S

DIE 1960ER

LES ANNÉES 1960

THURSDAY, AUGUST 6, 1962

Having left high school two years earlier and relocated from the mostly rural St. Ann Parish, where he grew up, 17-year-old Bob Marley—who made his singing debut in 1959 at a talent contest—is brought to the attention of Kingston, Jamaica, label owner, producer, and restaurateur Leslie Kong by singers Jimmy Cliff and Derrick Morgan. Marley records the original pop song *Judge Not* for Kong's Beverley's Records; it is credited to Robert Marley. His next song, *One Cup Of Coffee*, is credited to Bobby Martell.

Der 17-jährige Bob Marley, der zum ersten Mal 1959 bei einem Talentwettbewerb aufgetreten ist, hat zwei Jahre zuvor die Schule abgebrochen und die ländliche Gegend St. Ann Parish, wo er aufgewachsen ist, verlassen. Auf Vermittlung von Jimmy Cliff und Derrick Morgan erregt er die Aufmerksamkeit des Plattenfirmeninhabers, Produzenten und Restaurantbesitzers Leslie Kong. Marley nimmt den selbst geschriebenen Popsong *Judge Not* für Kongs Label Beverley's Records auf, sein Name wird mit Robert Marley angegeben. Bei seiner nächsten Single *One Cup Of Coffee* wird ein Bobby Martell als Interpret verzeichnet.

Bob Marley est âgé de 17 ans ; il a quitté le lycée et son village reculé des montagnes de Saint Ann deux ans plus tôt, après avoir fait ses débuts de chanteur lors d'un radio-crochet en 1959. Repéré par les chanteurs Jimmy Cliff et Derrick Morgan, ces derniers parlent de lui au producteur et restaurateur Leslie Kong, originaire de Kingston. Marley enregistre la chanson pop *Judge Not* pour la maison de disques de Kong, Beverley's Records, sous le nom de Robert Marley. Son titre suivant, *One Cup Of Coffee*, sort sous le nom de Bobby Martell.

Jamaica celebrates its independence after more than 300 years of British rule. / Jamaika feiert nach über 300 Jahren unter britischer Herrschaft seine Unabhängigkeit. / La Jamaïque célèbre son indépendance après plus de 300 ans de domination britannique.

1963

Under the tutelage of Joe Higgs, Marley forms a band with childhood friend Bunny Livingston from the Trench Town ghetto of West Kingston, Winston McIntosh, Junior Braithwaite, Cherry Green, and Beverly Kelso.

Unter Mithilfe von Joe Higgs gründet Marley mit seinen Jugendfreunden Bunny Livingston, Winston McIntosh, Junior Braithwaite, Cherry Green und Beverly Kelso aus dem Ghetto Trench Town in West Kingston eine Band.

Sous la houlette de Joe Higgs, Marley forme un groupe avec Bunny Livingston, son ami d'enfance du ghetto de Trench Town, dans West Kingston, ainsi que Winston McIntosh, Junior Braithwaite, Cherry Green et Beverly Kelso.

DECEMBER 1963

Local percussionist Alvin "Seeco" Patterson brings the group to audition for top Kingston producer Clement Seymour "Sir Coxsone" Dodd, owner of the Studio One label, with whom they will begin a prolific two-year recording relationship in 1964. They soon decide upon the name The Wailers, with McIntosh and Livingston also changing their names to become Peter Tosh and Bunny Wailer.

Der Perkussionist Alvin „Seeco" Patterson vermittelt ein Vorspiel der jungen Band beim wichtigsten Produzenten in Kingston, Clement Seymour „Sir Coxsone" Dodd, Inhaber des Labels Studio One. Ab 1964 entstehen in einer zweijährigen fruchtbaren Zusammenar-

beit zahlreiche Platteneinspielungen. Relativ bald fällt die Entscheidung für den Namen The Wailers, McIntosh und Livingston ändern ihre Namen in Peter Tosh und Bunny Wailer um.

Le percussionniste jamaïcain Alvin « Seeco » Patterson permet au groupe d'auditionner pour le plus gros producteur de Kingston, Clement Seymour alias « Sir Coxsone » Dodd, propriétaire du label Studio One. 1964 marque le début d'une collaboration fructueuse entre le groupe et la maison de disques. Le groupe prend le nom de The Wailers, tandis que McIntosh et Livingston se rebaptisent respectivement Peter Tosh et Bunny Wailer.

"Sir Coxsone" Dodd

1964

The Wailers' first Studio One single, *Simmer Down*, tops the chart in Jamaica and eventually sells an estimated 80,000 copies on the island. (The group will cut some 80 sides for Studio One between now and 1966—notably *Put It On*, *The Ten Commandments Of Love*, and *Love And Affection*.) Spending most of their time recording, they will play a handful of gigs during the year at the Ward, Palace, and Majestic theaters in Kingston. Before the year is out, however, Braithwaite will depart for the United States.

Die erste Single der Wailers bei Studio One, *Simmer Down*, schafft es an die Spitze der Charts in Jamaika und verkauft sich geschätzte 80.000 Mal auf der Insel. Die Bandmitglieder spielen bis 1966 um die 40 Singles für Studio One ein – erwähnenswert sind *Put It On*, *The Ten Commandments Of Love* und *Love And Affection*. Sie verbringen die meiste Zeit im Plattenstudio und haben im Laufe des Jahres nur einige wenige Auftritte in den Theatern Ward, Palace und Majestic in Kingston. Braithwaite wandert noch vor Jahresende in die USA aus.

Le premier single des Wailers pour Studio One, *Simmer Down*, est en tête des ventes en Jamaïque, où quelque 80 000 disques sont écoulés. (Le groupe enregistrera environ 80 titres en deux ans pour Studio One – notamment *Put It On*, *The Ten Commandments Of Love* et *Love And Affection*.) Les Wailers passent presque tout leur temps en studio et ne donnent qu'une poignée de concerts à Kingston au cours de l'année : au Ward Theatre, au Palace Theatre et au Majestic Theatre. Braithwaite embarque pour les États-Unis.

Ward Theatre, Kingston

"Me only have one ambition, y'know. I only have one thing I really like to see happen. I like to see mankind live together—black, white, Chinese, everyone—that's all."

„Ich habe nur ein großes Ziel und will im Grunde nur eine Sache von ganzem Herzen: Ich will, dass alle Menschen friedlich zusammenleben - Schwarze, Weiße, Chinesen, alle - sonst nichts."

« Je n'ai qu'une seule ambition. Il n'y a qu'une chose qui me tient véritablement à cœur : que l'humanité vive en bonne intelligence - les Noirs, les Blancs, les Chinois, tout le monde. Voilà tout. »

BOB MARLEY

1965

Now down to a core of Marley, Tosh, and Wailer, The Wailers record covers of The Beatles' *And I Love Her*, Tom Jones' *What's New Pussycat?*, and Irving Berlin's seasonal standard *White Christmas*. They close the year with five records in the Jamaican Top 10.

Die Wailers bestehen jetzt nur noch aus den drei Mitgliedern Marley, Tosh und Wailer und covern den Beatles-Song *And I Love Her*, Tom Jones' *What's New Pussycat?* und Irving Berlins Weihnachtsschlager *White Christmas*. Am Ende des Jahres haben sie fünf Platten in den jamaikanischen Top Ten.

Les Wailers, réduits à Marley, Tosh et Wailer, enregistrent leurs versions de *And I Love Her* des Beatles, *What's New Pussycat?* de Tom Jones et du classique de Noël *White Christmas* d'Irving Berlin. Ils terminent l'année avec cinq disques dans le Top 10 jamaïcain.

FRIDAY, FEBRUARY 11, 1966

The day after marrying Rita Anderson, a member of The Soulettes, Marley leaves Kingston for the United States to visit his mother in Wilmington, Delaware, finding work as a cleaner at the Hotel DuPont. He spends an unhappy eight months in the United States; the trip ends with him receiving a notice from the Selective Service Bureau informing him that he must register for the draft.

Einen Tag nach seiner Eheschließung mit Rita Anderson, Sängerin bei The Soulettes, reist Marley in die USA, um seine Mutter in Wilmington, Delaware, zu besuchen. Er findet Arbeit als Putzhilfe im Hotel DuPont, verbringt acht unglückliche Monate in den Vereinigten Staaten und kehrt nach Hause zurück, als er eine Benachrichtigung vom Selective Service Bureau erhält, er solle sich zum amerikanischen Wehrdienst melden.

Le lendemain de son mariage avec Rita Anderson, membre des Soulettes, Marley part aux États-Unis pour rejoindre sa mère à Wilmington, dans le Delaware. Il y passe huit mois difficiles, vivant de petits boulots, notamment comme homme de ménage à l'hôtel DuPont. Son séjour s'achève lorsqu'il reçoit sa lettre de conscription du Selective Service Bureau.

THURSDAY, APRIL 21, 1966

Emperor Haile Selassie I of Ethiopia makes a state visit to Jamaica. More than 100,000 Jamaicans greet him at Palisadoes Airport in Kingston. Born Tafari Makonnen in 1892, Selassie has been anointed by the Rastafarian movement that began in Jamaica in the 1930s. Although her husband is in the United States, Rita Marley—and members of The Wailers—are deeply moved by Selassie's visit, and they all convert to the Rastafarian philosophy, which Bob himself will also adopt upon his return to his homeland.

Kaiser Haile Selassie I. von Äthiopien weilt auf Staatsbesuch in Jamaika. Über 100.000 Jamaikaner begrüßen ihn am Palisadoes Airport in Kingston. Selassie, 1892 als Tafari Makonnen geboren, ist für die Rastafari-Bewegung, die in den 1930er Jahren auf Jamaika entstand, der wiedergekehrte Messias. Rita Marley und die Mitglieder der Wailers sind von Haile Selassies Besuch tief bewegt und bekehren sich zur Rastafari-Philosophie, die Bob Marley bei seiner Rückkehr aus Amerika ebenfalls annimmt.

L'Empereur Haïlé Sélassié Ier d'Éthiopie arrive en Jamaïque pour une visite d'État. Plus de 100 000 Jamaïcains l'accueillent à l'aéroport Palisadoes de Kingston. Né en 1892, Sélassié (Ras Tafari Makonnen) a reçu l'onction du mouvement rastafari apparu en Jamaïque dans les années 1930. Rita Marley et les autres membres des Wailers sont profondément émus par la visite de Sélassié et se convertissent tous à la « philosophie » rasta, que Bob embrasse à son tour dès son retour d'Amérique.

OCTOBER 1966

Marley returns to Kingston with his first electric guitar and $700 in savings, with which he sets up his own Wail'n Soul'm label. He and Rita move into her aunt Viola's Greenwich Park Road home, where during the day they sell 45 rpm singles out of a cashier's booth at the front of the house.

Marley kehrt mit seiner ersten elektrischen Gitarre und 700 zusammengesparten Dollar nach Kingston zurück und gründet sein eigenes Label Wail'n Soul'm.

Rita und er ziehen in das Haus ihrer Tante Viola an der Greenwich Park Road, wo sie tagsüber in einer Bude vor dem Haus Singles verkaufen.

Marley revient à Kingston avec sa première guitare électrique et 700 dollars d'économies, avec lesquels il monte son propre label, Wail'n Soul'm. Le jeune couple s'installe sur Greenwich Park Road chez Viola, la tante de Rita ; pendant la journée, ils vendent leurs 45 tours depuis un stand installé devant son domicile.

SUNDAY, JANUARY 7, 1968

Rasta elder Mortimo Planno introduces Marley to American singer Johnny Nash at a grounation in Kingston. Nash, in Jamaica looking for talent to break in the United States, has already had a recommendation from deejay Neville Willoughby. Nash and his manager, Danny Sims, sign The Wailers to a publishing and production deal with their company, JAD. Bunny Wailer is in the midst of a 15-month prison sentence after being convicted of marijuana possession.

Der Rasta-Älteste Mortimo Planno macht Marley bei einer Grounation-Feier in Kingston mit dem amerikanischen Sänger Johnny Nash bekannt. Nash sucht auf Jamaika nach Talenten, die er in den USA vermarkten kann, und hatte bereits eine Empfehlung von DJ Neville Willoughby erhalten. Nash und sein Manager, Danny Sims, schließen einen Veröffentlichungs- und Produktionsvertrag zwischen The Wailers und der Plattenfirma JAD ab. Bunny Wailer sitzt wegen Marihuanabesitz 15 Monate im Gefängnis.

Le sage rasta Mortimo Planno présente Marley au chanteur américain Johnny Nash à l'occasion d'une célébration rituelle appelée *grounation*, organisée à Kingston. Nash, qui se trouve en Jamaïque pour débusquer de jeunes talents susceptibles de percer aux États-Unis, a déjà entendu parler de Marley par le DJ Neville Willoughby. Nash et son manager Danny Sims signent pour leur label JAD un contrat d'édition et de production exclusive avec les Wailers. Pendant ce temps-là, Bunny Wailer purge une peine de quinze mois de prison pour détention de marijuana.

Johnny Nash

1968

With Bunny Wailer having served out his sentence, the group begins recording a series of demos for Danny Sims—an estimated eighty-plus over the next four years—while simultaneously recording with Lee Perry. The deal with Sims pays them $50 a week each.

Als Bunny Wailer seine Haftstrafe abgesessen hat, beginnt die Band mit einer Reihe von Demoaufnahmen für Danny Sims – schätzungsweise an die neunzig im Laufe der nächsten vier Jahre – und arbeitet gleichzeitig auch mit Lee Perry im Tonstudio.

Bei dem Deal mit Danny Sims verdient jeder 50 Dollar pro Woche.

Après avoir purgé sa peine, Bunny Wailer retrouve le groupe avec lequel il commence l'enregistrement d'une longue série de maquettes (estimées à plus de 80 au cours des quatre années qui suivent); sous contrat avec Danny Sims, chacun des membres empoche 50 dollars par semaine. Parallèlement, les Wailers enregistrent pour Lee Perry.

1969

Marley moves back to Wilmington during the summer to earn some money. He finds work as a forklift driver on a night shift in a warehouse, and then as an assembly-line worker in the Chrysler plant.

Marley geht den Sommer über wieder nach Wilmington, um Geld zu verdienen. Er findet einen Job als Gabelstaplerfahrer in einer Lagerhalle und anschließend als Fließbandarbeiter bei Chrysler.

Marley passe l'été à Wilmington pour gagner de l'argent. Il travaille comme cariste de nuit dans un entrepôt puis sur les chaînes de montage d'une usine Chrysler.

THE 1970^S

DIE 1970ER

LES ANNÉES 1970

1970

The Wailers turn to Leslie Kong, recording several tracks with him, which he releases as ***The Best Of The Wailers***. Bunny Wailer tells Kong that, if this is the best of The Wailers to him, he must be going to die soon. In August of 1971, at the age of 38, Kong suffers a fatal heart attack. The Wailers hook up with Lee "Scratch" Perry, with whom they record a number of reggae standards, including *Soul Rebel, Duppy Conqueror, 400 Years,* and *Small Axe.* Perry also teams them with his hit-making studio band, The Upsetters, driven by the bass-and-drum rhythm section of Aston "Family Man" Barrett and his brother, Carlton.

Die Wailers nehmen mit Produzent Leslie Kong mehrere Stücke auf, die er als ***The Best Of The Wailers*** herausbringt. Bunny Wailer soll zu Kong gesagt haben, dass er wohl bald sterben werde, wenn das schon das Beste der Wailers für ihn sei. Im August 1971 stirbt Kong im Alter von 38 Jahren an einem Herzinfarkt. Vom selben Monat an arbeiten The Wailers mit Lee „Scratch" Perry zusammen, mit dem sie eine ganze Reihe von Reggaestandards aufnehmen, darunter *Soul Rebel, Duppy Conqueror, 400 Years* und *Small Axe.* Perry bringt sie auch mit seiner Hit-erprobten Studioband The Upsetters zusammen, deren stärkstes Element die Bass- und Schlagzeug-Rhythmusgruppe ist, bestehend aus Aston „Family Man" Barrett und seinem Bruder Carlton.

Les Wailers se tournent vers Leslie Kong, avec lequel ils enregistrent plusieurs titres pour l'album ***The Best Of The Wailers***. Bunny Wailer dit à Kong que s'il pense qu'il s'agit là du «meilleur des Wailers», alors ses jours sont comptés. En août 1971, à l'âge de 38 ans, Kong meurt d'une crise cardiaque. Au même moment, les Wailers rencontrent Lee «Scratch» Perry, avec lequel ils enregistrent de nombreux standards du reggae, dont *Soul Rebel, Duppy Conqueror, 400 Years* et *Small Axe.* Parallèlement, Perry les met en relation avec son célèbre groupe de studio, The Upsetters, conduit par la section rythmique basse-batterie d'Aston «Family Man» Barrett et de son frère Carlton.

1971

After an acrimonious falling-out with Perry in April, the group starts its own label, Tuff Gong (Marley's nickname). Marley and Rita move to Wilmington for a while and then to New York, where they spend time with Johnny Nash and his wife. Marley is offered a deal to help Nash write songs for "Want So Much To Believe," a movie in which Nash is appearing. Rita returns home as Marley heads to Sweden to continue working with Nash.

Nach einem erbitterten Streit mit Perry gründet die Band im April ihr eigenes Label Tuff Gong (Marleys Spitzname). Marley und Rita ziehen für eine Weile nach Wilmington und später nach New York, wo sie Zeit mit Johnny Nash und seiner Frau verbringen.

Marley erhält das Angebot, Nash beim Schreiben von Songs für den Film „Want So Much to Believe" zu helfen, in dem Nash mitspielt. Rita kehrt nach Hause zurück, Marley fährt nach Schweden, um dort mit Nash weiterzuarbeiten.

Après une rupture acrimonieuse avec Perry en avril, le groupe crée son label indépendant, Tuff Gong (le surnom de Marley). Marley et Rita s'installent quelque temps à Wilmington puis à New York, où ils fréquentent Johnny Nash et son épouse. Nash propose à Marley de l'aider à composer la musique du long métrage « Want So Much to Believe » dans lequel il fait une apparition. Rita rentre en Jamaïque et Marley part en Suède pour travailler avec Nash.

THURSDAY, JANUARY 27, 1972

Marley flies from Stockholm to London and immediately moves into 34 Ridgmount Gardens, Bloomsbury, WC1, with Johnny Nash's entourage. He will record *Reggae On Broadway* with Nash's band for CBS Records in April, and by August will be joined by The Wailers to back Nash—who is fusing reggae into his repertoire—on a United Kingdom tour of secondary schools. Three Marley songs appear on Johnny Nash's *I Can See Clearly Now* album. Marley will also make a showcase appearance at CBS Records' annual conference at the Grosvenor House Hotel.

Marley fliegt von Stockholm nach London und wohnt zusammen mit Johnny Nashs Gefolge in dem Apartment 34 Ridgmount Gardens, Bloomsbury, WC1. Im April nimmt er mit Nashs Band für CBS Records *Reggae On Broadway* auf, im August stoßen auch The Wailers dazu und begleiten Nash, der Reggae in sein Repertoire aufnimmt, auf einer Tour mit Konzerten in englischen Oberschulen. Auf Johnny Nashs Album *I Can See Clearly Now* erscheinen drei Marley-Kompositionen. Marley tritt bei einem Showcase im Grosvenor House Hotel bei der Jahresversammlung von CBS Records auf.

Marley quitte Stockholm pour Londres, où il emménage avec l'entourage de Johnny Nash au 34 Ridgmount Gardens, dans le quartier de Bloomsbury. En avril, il enregistre *Reggae On Broadway* avec le groupe de Nash pour CBS Records. En août, il est rejoint par les Wailers pour accompagner Nash – qui intègre le reggae à son répertoire – lors d'une tournée dans des écoles britanniques. Trois chansons de Marley figurent sur l'album *I Can See Clearly Now* de Johnny Nash. Marley se produit à la soirée annuelle organisée par CBS Records au Grosvenor House Hotel.

OCTOBER 1972

After Brent Clarke, a promoter who worked *Reggae On Broadway*, gets a Wailers demo to Island Records founder Chris Blackwell, the band secures an album deal. Blackwell—himself a white Jamaican—signs them to a long-term recording agreement via Tuff Gong, paying them an initial £4,000 advance. The group returns to Jamaica to record the first album. Following recording sessions at Harry J's studio in Kingston, Marley returns to London with the tapes at Blackwell's behest. Southern rocker Wayne Perkins and Texan John "Rabbit" Bundrick sweeten the record with guitar and keyboard overdubs.

Nachdem Brent Clarke, ein Promoter, der an *Reggae On Broadway* mitgearbeitet hat, dem Gründer des Labels Island Records Chris Blackwell ein Wailers-Demoband in die Hand gedrückt hat, schließt die Band einen Plattenvertrag mit ihm ab. Blackwell, ein weißer Jamaikaner, verpflichtet sie über Tuff Gong zu einem langjährigen Plattenvertrag und zahlt ihnen einen Vorschuss von 4.000 Pfund. Die Band kehrt nach Jamaika zurück, um das erste Album für ihn aufzunehmen. Nach Abschluss der Aufnahmesession im Studio Harry J in Kingston kehrt Marley auf Blackwells Anordnung mit den Bändern nach London zurück. Dort werden Overdubs des Südstaatenrockers Wayne Perkins und des Texaners John „Rabbit" Bundrick an Gitarre und Keyboard aufgenommen und dazugemischt.

Brent Clarke, un organisateur de spectacles qui a travaillé sur *Reggae On Broadway*, apporte une bande démo des Wailers au fondateur d'Island Records, Chris Blackwell, lequel signe sur le champ un contrat pour un album avec le groupe. Blackwell – lui-même Jamaïcain blanc – leur offre un contrat d'enregistrement à long terme en association avec Tuff Gong, assorti d'une avance de 4 000 livres. Le groupe retourne en Jamaïque pour enregistrer son premier album. Lorsque les séances sont achevées au studio de Harry J, à Kingston, Marley se rend à Londres pour y remettre les bandes à Blackwell. Le rocker sudiste Wayne Perkins et le Texan John « Rabbit » Bundrick adoucissent l'ensemble en y ajoutant guitare et clavier.

"Life is one big road with lots of signs, so when you riding through the ruts, don't complicate your mind. Flee from hate, mischief and jealousy. Don't bury your thoughts, put your vision to reality. Wake up and live."

„Das Leben ist eine lange Straße mit einer Menge Schildern, und wenn man durch die ausgefahrenen Rillen rumpelt, dann sollte man sich keine zu komplizierten Gedanken machen. Meide Hass, Eifersucht und Unrecht. Versteck deine Gedanken nicht, lass deine Sicht der Welt Wirklichkeit werden. Wach auf und lebe.“

« La vie est une longue route jalonnée de panneaux indicateurs, alors tu sais, quand tu traces ta route, t'a pas besoin de te poser des tonnes de questions. Évite la haine, la jalousie, la méchanceté. Ne dissimule pas tes pensées, fais en sorte que ta vision du monde devienne réalité. Réveille-toi et vis. »

BOB MARLEY

FRIDAY, APRIL 13, 1973

The band's debut album for Island Records, **Catch A Fire**, is released. The landmark nine-track set, mainly written by Marley and featuring *Concrete Jungle, Slave Driver, Stir It Up*—a Top 20 hit for Johnny Nash in the United Kingdom last year and now about to peak in the United States—and *Kinky Reggae*, will bring reggae music into the mainstream, introducing the genre to a worldwide audience.

Das Debütalbum der Band für Island Records, **Catch A Fire**, kommt heraus. Die neun zum größten Teil von Marley geschriebenen Stücke werden Geschichte machen - auf der LP finden sich Titel wie *Concrete Jungle, Slave Driver, Kinky Reggae* und *Stir It Up* - ein Top-Twenty-Hit für Johnny Nash im Vorjahr in England, der jetzt in den USA ganz oben in den Charts mitmischt. Reggae wird zum Mainstream, ein weltweites Publikum wird zum ersten Mal auf dieses Genre aufmerksam.

Sortie de **Catch A Fire**, le premier album du groupe chez Island Records : les neuf titres, entrés dans la légende, ont presque tous été composés par Marley lui-même. Avec *Concrete Jungle, Slave Driver, Stir It Up* - une chanson que Johnny Nash avait fait entrer au Top 20 britannique un an plus tôt - et *Kinky Reggae*, le monde s'ouvre au reggae, qui séduit un public international.

FRIDAY, APRIL 27, 1973

The English leg of the group's "Catch A Fire" tour begins at the Coleman Club in Nottingham, Nottinghamshire. It will run through May 29, with an appearance at the Coach House in Southampton, Hampshire. During the tour, the band will make an appearance on BBC2 Television's revered "The Old Grey Whistle Test" and, on May 1, BBC Radio's "Top Gear."

Die Serie der Konzerte in Großbritannien auf der auf der Tournee „Catch A Fire" beginnt im Coleman Club in Nottingham, Nottinghamshire. Die Band tourt bis zum 29. Mai, auch ein Auftritt im Coach House in Southampton, Hampshire, ist dabei. Im Lauf der Tournee tritt die Band auch im Fernsehen auf, bei der beliebten BBC2-Sendung „The Old Grey Whistle Test" und am 1. Mai im BBC-Radio bei „Top Gear".

Le groupe entame la partie anglaise de la tournée « Catch A Fire » au Coleman Club de Nottingham. Elle fera halte notamment à la Coach House de Southampton (Hampshire) et s'achèvera le 29 mai. Le groupe fera une apparition dans la célèbre émission de la BBC2 « The Old Grey Whistle Test » ; le 1er mai, il se produira dans l'émission de radio « Top Gear » de la BBC.

WEDNESDAY, JULY 18, 1973
Following five dates at Paul's Mall in Boston,
Massachusetts, The Wailers—with Joe Higgs replacing
Bunny Wailer on the road and the addition of Earl
Lindo on keyboards—co-headline the first of six nights
with Bruce Springsteen and the E Street Band at
Max's Kansas City, a club in New York City.

Nach fünf Auftritten in Paul's Mall in Boston, Massachusetts, geben The Wailers das erste von sechs Konzerten – mit Joe Higgs als Tourersatz für Bunny Wailer
und zusätzlich Earl Lindo am Keyboard – zusammen
mit Bruce Springsteen und der E Street Band im Max's
Kansas City, einem Club in New York.

Après cinq dates au Paul's Mall de Boston (Massachusetts), les Wailers – avec Earl Lindo au clavier et
Joe Higgs en remplacement de Bunny Wailer – partagent l'affiche avec Bruce Springsteen et le E Street
Band dans un club new-yorkais, le Max's Kansas City.

FRIDAY, OCTOBER 19, 1973
The group plays the first of four hurriedly arranged
shows at the Matrix in San Francisco, replacing the
Sons of Champlin after being dropped five dates into
a 17-date U.S. tour opening for Sly and The Family
Stone. The Wailers' tour, in support of their new album,
Burnin', will move to England, where several dates will
be cancelled because of heavy snow. The revised
itinerary will close in Northampton on November 30,
after which Tosh will quit the lineup.

Die Band tritt beim ersten von vier hastig arrangier-
ten Konzerten im Matrix in San Francisco auf, wo sie
die Sons of Champlin ersetzen, nachdem ihre Teilnahme bei fünf Konzerten einer 17-Tage-Tour in den
USA als Vorgruppe von Sly and The Family Stone
gestrichen wurde. Danach geht die Promo-Tour der
Wailers für ihr neues Album **Burnin'** in England weiter,
wo mehrere Termine wegen starker Schneefälle abgesagt werden. Nach dem Ende der Tournee am 30.
November in Northampton verlässt Tosh die Band.

Le groupe remplace au pied levé les Sons of Champlin pour quatre concerts au Matrix de San Francisco,
après avoir été évincé de la tournée américaine de 17
dates de Sly and The Family Stone, dont il devait assu-
rer la première partie pour cinq concerts. La tournée
des Wailers pour leur nouvel album, **Burnin'**, traverse à
nouveau l'Atlantique, mais plusieurs dates anglaises
sont annulées à cause d'abondantes chutes de neige.
La tournée s'achèvera le 30 novembre à Northampton,
à l'issue de laquelle Tosh quittera le groupe.

1974

The Wailers return to the studio early in the year to begin work on what will be ***Natty Dread***. Tosh and Wailer are no longer members of the band, which now includes Al Anderson on guitar, Bernard "Touter" Harvey on keyboards, Alvin "Seeco" Patterson on percussion, and I-Three—comprising Marley's wife, Rita, Judy Mowatt, and Marcia Griffiths—as backing vocalists.

Anfang des Jahres kehren The Wailers ins Plattenstudio zurück und beginnen mit der Arbeit an ***Natty Dread***. Tosh und Wailer sind nicht mehr mit von der Partie, die Band besteht jetzt aus Al Anderson an der Gitarre, Bernard „Touter" Harvey am Keyboard, Alvin „Seeco" Patterson, Percussion, und den I-Three als Backgroundsängerinnen – Marleys Frau Rita, Judy Mowatt und Marcia Griffiths.

Les Wailers retournent en studio en début d'année pour travailler à leur nouvel album, ***Natty Dread***. Tosh et Wailer ne font plus partie du groupe, lequel, en revanche, a été rejoint par Al Anderson à la guitare, Bernard « Touter » Harvey au clavier et Alvin « Seeco » Patterson aux percussions et par les I-Three – Rita Marley, Judy Mowatt et Marcia Griffiths – aux chœurs.

TUESDAY, MAY 28, 1974

Marley opens for Marvin Gaye at the Carib Theatre in Kingston, Jamaica. He meets Don Taylor, the organizer of the event and current manager of Little Anthony and The Imperials. Marley persuades the Jamaican-born Taylor to become his manager.

Marley bestreitet das Vorprogramm für Marvin Gaye im Carib Theatre in Kingston, Jamaika. Er lernt den Veranstalter Don Taylor kennen, Manager von Little Anthony and the Imperials. Marley überredet den auf Jamaika geborenen Taylor, sein Manager zu werden.

Marley assure la première partie de Marvin Gaye au Carib Theatre de Kingston. Il rencontre Don Taylor, l'organisateur de l'événement, alors manager de Little Anthony and the Imperials. Marley convainc ce Jamaïcain de souche de devenir son agent.

SATURDAY, SEPTEMBER 14, 1974

Eric Clapton provides Marley with his first United States chart topper as *I Shot The Sheriff* hits number 1. Originally recorded for The Wailers' album **Burnin'**, Clapton's cover version becomes a global smash, bringing Marley's music to a broader international audience.

Eric Claptons Coverversion von *I Shot The Sheriff* wird Marleys erster Nummer-1-Hit in den US-Charts. Das ursprünglich auf dem Wailers-Album **Burnin'** herausgekommene Stück wird in Claptons Interpretation ein weltweiter Megahit und macht Marleys Musik einem breiteren internationalen Publikum bekannt.

Eric Clapton offre à Marley son premier gros succès international : *I Shot The Sheriff*, enregistré à l'origine pour figurer dans l'album **Burnin'**, atteint la 1ʳᵉ place des charts américains. La reprise de Clapton fera le tour du monde, contribuant ainsi à populariser la musique de Marley auprès d'un large public international.

Eric Clapton

THURSDAY, JUNE 5, 1975

The group, with Tyrone Downie taking over for Bernard Harvey, begins another slew of dates in North America in support of its **Natty Dread** album, starting with a show at the Diplomat Hotel in Miami, Florida. Four dates at the Boarding House in San Francisco, California, will lead promoter Bill Graham to book the band at the Paramount Theatre in Oakland, California. The tour will end on July 13 with the last of four shows at the Roxy Theater in Los Angeles, California.

Die Band mit Bernard Harvey anstelle von Tyrone Downie gibt eine Reihe von Konzerten in Nordamerika, um ihr neues Album **Natty Dread** zu promoten. Der Auftakt findet im Diplomat Hotel in Miami, Florida,

statt. Nach vier Auftritten im Boarding House in San Francisco, Kalifornien, bucht Veranstalter Bill Graham die Band für das Paramount Theatre in Oakland, Kalifornien. Die Tour endet am 13. Juli mit vier Konzerten im Roxy Theater in Los Angeles, Kalifornien.

Le groupe inaugure une nouvelle tournée nord-américaine pour la promotion de l'album **Natty Dread**, avec Tyrone Downie à la place de Bernard Harvey, par un concert à l'Hôtel Diplomat de Miami. Ses quatre dates à la Boarding House de San Francisco convainquent le tourneur Bill Graham de l'engager pour un concert au Paramount Theatre d'Oakland (Californie). La tournée s'achève le 13 juillet avec le dernier de quatre concerts au Roxy Theater de Los Angeles.

MECCA **LYCEUM** The Strand, London WC2

A.L.E. Limited in association with Island Artists
present

BOB MARLEY and the WAILERS

and Special Guests

THIRD WORLD

on FRIDAY 18th JULY 1975 at 7.30 p.m.

Tickets £1.50

THURSDAY, JULY 17, 1975

Marley and The Wailers perform the first of two shows at the Lyceum Ballroom in London. A combination of today's and tomorrow's shows will compose the concert album to be released on Island Records in December as the seminal performance set *Live!* Two further concerts will be performed in Birmingham and Manchester. An uplifting testament to Marley and his band's magical onstage presence, *Live!* contains an energetic version of *I Shot The Sheriff* and a deeply moving rendition of *No Woman, No Cry* (originally featured on the studio album *Natty Dread*). Released as a single in September, *No Woman, No Cry* peaks at number 22 on the United Kingdom charts but fails to score in the United States altogether, though it will subsequently become one of Marley's most revered songs and a radio staple around the world.

Marley and The Wailers geben zwei Konzerte im Lyceum Ballroom in London. Aus den Konzerten an diesem und dem nächsten Tag wird das Album *Live!* zusammengeschnitten. Dieser musikalische Meilenstein erscheint im Dezember bei Island Records. Zwei weitere Konzerte finden in Birmingham und Manchester statt. Das Album *Live!* ist ein Zeugnis für die magische Bühnenpräsenz von Marley und seiner Band und

enthält eine energiegeladene Fassung von *I Shot The Sheriff* und eine bewegende Version von dem Song *No Woman, No Cry* (der ursprünglich auf dem Studioalbum *Natty Dread* herausgekommen ist). *No Woman, No Cry* kommt im September als Single heraus und schafft es in England auf Platz 22. In den USA erreicht der Song zunächst keine Chartplatzierung, er entwickelt sich aber später zu einem von Marleys beliebtesten und weltweit im Radio gesendeten Evergreens.

Marley et les Wailers donnent deux soirées au Lyceum Ballroom de Londres. Ces concerts et les précédents fournissent la matière de l'album *Live!* qu'Island Records sortira en décembre. Le groupe se produit à Birmingham et Manchester. *Live!*, témoignage exaltant de la présence magique sur scène de Marley et de son groupe, inclut une interprétation énergique de *I Shot The Sheriff* et une version très émouvante de *No Woman, No Cry*. Ce titre, déjà présent sur l'album *Natty Dread*, ressort en 45 tours et se hisse à la 22e place du classement britannique, mais il ne convainc pas le public américain ; il deviendra pourtant une des chansons les plus populaires de Marley, diffusée encore aujourd'hui sur les ondes du monde entier.

WEDNESDAY, AUGUST 27, 1975
Haile Selassie passes away. Marley is in the midst of cutting his new album at Harry J Studio in Kingston. Soon after the Emperor's death, Marley will record *Jah Live* and *War*—the lyrics of which are taken from a speech given to the United Nations in October 1963 by the Emperor. Marley will increasingly invoke Selassie's name and message in future concerts.

Haile Selassie stirbt. Marley ist gerade bei den Aufnahmen zu seinem neuen Album im Harry J Studio in Kingston. Kurz nach dem Ableben des Kaisers spielt Marley *Jah Live* und *War* ein - der Text dieses Liedes entstammt einer Rede, die der äthiopische Kaiser im Oktober 1963 vor den Vereinten Nationen gehalten hat. Marley wird von diesem Tag an bei seinen Konzerten häufiger von Selassie und seiner Botschaft sprechen.

Mort d'Hailé Sélassié. Marley est en plein mixage de son nouvel album au Studio Harry J de Kingston. Peu après le décès de l'empereur, Marley enregistre *Jah Live* et *War*, dont les paroles sont empruntées à un discours prononcé par Sélassié aux Nations unies en octobre 1963. Marley invoquera de plus en plus souvent le nom et le message de l'Empereur au cours de ses futurs concerts.

SUNDAY, AUGUST 31, 1975
The group makes its United States television debut
on CBS Television's "The Manhattan Transfer Show,"
performing *Kinky Reggae.*
Marley and The Wailers sind zum ersten Mal im
amerikanischen Fernsehen zu sehen, der Sender CBS
strahlt die „Manhattan Transfer Show" aus, bei der sie
Kinky Reggae spielen.
Pour sa première apparition à la télévision américaine sur CBS, dans « The Manhattan Transfer Show »,
le groupe joue *Kinky Reggae.*

"Buckle your seat belts nice and tight. Be prepared for the heavenly
flight. It's the big one, the big bad boss sound from Trench Town, Jamaica,
the Trench Town experience, Bob Marley and The Wailers."
„Schnallen Sie sich gut fest. Legen Sie die Sitzgurte an für einen himmlischen
Flug. Machen Sie sich bereit, hier kommt der große, wahnsinnige Sound aus
Trench Town, Jamaika, heben Sie ab, hier sind Bob Marley and The Wailers."
« Attachez vos ceintures. Préparez-vous à atteindre le nirvana. Voici le grand,
le gros son venu tout droit de Trench Town, en Jamaïque. Venez vibrer avec
Bob Marley et les Wailers ! »
ANNOUNCER, THE MANHATTAN TRANSFER SHOW

SEPTEMBER 1975
A longtime soccer fan, whose favorite team is
Brazil's Santos, Marley is playing in Trench Town, when
a player, wearing spikes, steps on his foot.

Beim Fußballspielen in Trench Town tritt ein Mit-
spieler Marley, langjähriger Fan der brasilianischen
Mannschaft Santos, mit seinen Stollen auf den Fuß.

Grand amateur de ballon rond et fervent supporter
de l'équipe de Santos, au Brésil, Marley se fait écraser
le pied par un joueur chaussé de crampons au cours
d'une partie de football à Trench Town.

"Football is a whole skill to itself. A whole world.
A whole universe to itself. Me love it because you have to be skillful to play it!
Freedom! Football is freedom."
„Fußball ist eine Kunst für sich. Eine Welt für sich. Ein Universum für sich.
Ich liebe Fußball, weil man viel können muss, um gut zu spielen!
Freiheit! Fußball ist Freiheit!"
« Le football est une technique, un art à part entière. Tout un monde.
Tout un univers à lui seul. Nous adorons le foot parce qu'il faut être habile
pour y jouer ! Liberté ! Le football, c'est la liberté. »
BOB MARLEY

SATURDAY, OCTOBER 4, 1975

Marley and The Wailers play a concert at Kingston's National Stadium to benefit the Jamaican Institute for the Blind, opening for the bill-topper, Stevie Wonder, with whom Marley sings *I Shot The Sheriff* and *Superstition*. It is the last time the trio of Marley, Tosh, and Wailer performs together.

Marley and The Wailers spielen im National Stadium in Kingston bei einem Benefizkonzert für die jamaikanische Blindenschule als Vorband von Stevie Wonder, mit dem Marley zusammen *I Shot The Sheriff* und *Superstition* singt. Es ist das letzte Mal, dass Marley, Tosh und Wailer zusammen auf der Bühne stehen.

Marley et les Wailers jouent au National Stadium de Kingston au profit de l'Institut jamaïcain des Aveugles, en première partie de Stevie Wonder, avec lequel Marley chante *I Shot The Sheriff* et *Superstition*. C'est la dernière fois que Marley, Tosh et Wailer se produisent ensemble sur scène.

FRIDAY, OCTOBER 10, 1975

An internal Jamaican Tourist Board memo contends that "when we promote reggae music we are promoting an aspect of Jamaican culture which is bound to draw attention to some of the harsher circumstances of our lives."

Ein internes Memorandum des jamaikanischen Fremdenverkehrsamtes stellt fest: „Wenn wir für Reggaemusik werben, fördern wir einen Aspekt der jamaikanischen Kultur, der die Aufmerksamkeit auf die schwierigeren Bedingungen des Lebens hier lenken könnte."

Une note interne du Bureau jamaïcain du tourisme : « Lorsque nous faisons la promotion de la musique reggae, nous faisons la promotion d'un aspect de la culture jamaïcaine qui attirera l'attention sur certaines des facettes les plus difficiles de nos vies. »

FRIDAY, APRIL 23, 1976

With the release of **Rastaman Vibration** (which will become the group's highest-charting United States album, peaking at number 8) a week away, Marley and The Wailers set out on an extended tour to promote the album, starting at the Tower Theater in Upper Darby, Pennsylvania. The North American leg will come to a close in Miami, Florida, in June. With Marley's political compositions becoming increasingly controversial, the Jamaican government initiates a radio ban on four of the tracks: *Crazy Baldheads, Who The Cap Fit, War,* and *Rat Race.*

Eine Woche vor der Veröffentlichung des Albums **Rastaman Vibration** (mit dem die Gruppe ihre höchste Platzierung in den US-Album-Charts erreichen wird, nämlich Rang 8) starten Marley and The Wailers zu einer ausgedehnten Tournee, um das neue Album zu promoten; der Auftakt findet im Tower Theater in Upper Darby, Pennsylvania, statt. Im Juni findet der nordamerikanische Abschnitt der Tour in Miami, Florida, seinen Abschluss. Marleys Songtexte werden politisch zunehmend radikaler und die jamaikanische Regierung verhängt über vier Titel Radiozensur: *Crazy Baldheads, Who The Cap Fit, War* und *Rat Race.*

À une semaine de la sortie de **Rastaman Vibration** (l'album le mieux classé du groupe aux États-Unis, puisqu'il atteindra la 8ᵉ place), Marley et les Wailers partent pour une longue tournée, qui commence au Tower Theater d'Upper Darby (Pennsylvanie). La partie américaine du périple s'achève à Miami en juin. Les textes politiques de Marley étant de plus en plus agressifs, le gouvernement jamaïcain interdit la diffusion sur les ondes de quatre titres (*Crazy Baldheads, Who The Cap Fit, War* et *Rat Race*).

TUESDAY, JUNE 15 TO FRIDAY, JUNE 18, 1976

Following concerts in Germany, Sweden, the Netherlands, and France, the group plays six sold-out dates at London's Hammersmith Odeon. Seven shows will follow, including the "West Coast Rock Show" at Ninian Park in Cardiff, Wales.

Nach Konzerten in Deutschland, Schweden, den Niederlanden und Frankreich gibt die Band sechs völlig ausverkaufte Konzerte im Londoner Hammersmith Odeon. Darauf folgen noch sieben weitere Auftritte, unter anderem bei der „West Coast Rock Show" im Ninian Park in Cardiff, Wales.

Après des concerts en Allemagne, en Suède, aux Pays-Bas et en France, le groupe remplit le Hammersmith Odeon de Londres six soirs de suite. Sept autres dates suivront, notamment lors du « West Coast Rock Show » au Ninian Park de Cardiff, au Pays de Galles.

"Nothing had prepared me for the sheer power that Marley is able to generate ... I mean the kind of power to move people."

„Nichts hatte mich auf Marleys unglaubliche Ausstrahlung vorbereitet ... Er hat die Kraft, Menschen zu bewegen."

« Rien ne m'avait préparé à la puissance brute que Marley est capable de générer... Je parle d'une puissance qui fait bouger les gens. »

MICK FARREN, NME, JUNE 26, 1976

TUESDAY, NOVEMBER 2, 1976

An announcement is made from Jamaica House that a free concert called "Smile Jamaica," a collaboration between Marley and the cultural section of the Prime Minister's office, is to be held at the National Stadium in Kingston. Marley agrees to headline the event, and records the track *Smile Jamaica*, with Lee Perry coproducing. Despite assurances of its lack of political bias, Prime Minister Michael Manley calls a snap election to be held two weeks after the concert.

Das Jamaica House, Amtssitz des Premierministers, gibt bekannt, dass ein Konzert mit freiem Eintritt unter dem Motto „Smile Jamaica" im National Stadium in Kingston als Zusammenarbeit von Marley und der Kulturabteilung des Premierministers stattfinden soll. Marley gibt seine Zustimmung, als wichtigster Act auf-

zutreten, und nimmt mit Lee Perry als Koproduzent das Stück *Smile Jamaica* auf. Premierminister Michael Manley hatte zwar versichert, dass es politisch neutral zugehen würde, er ruft dann aber überraschend Neuwahlen für zwei Wochen nach dem Konzert aus.

Jamaica House annonce la tenue d'un concert gratuit au National Stadium de Kingston, « Smile Jamaica », une collaboration entre Marley et le département culturel des bureaux du Premier ministre. Marley accepte de participer à l'événement et enregistre le titre *Smile Jamaica*, coproduit par Lee Perry. Malgré sa promesse de ne pas exploiter sa présence politiquement, le Premier ministre Michael Manley organise une élection anticipée deux semaines après le concert.

FRIDAY, DECEMBER 3, 1976
An attempt is made on Marley's life when five gunmen burst into his home at 56 Hope Road in Kingston at just after 9:30 P.M. Two white Datsun saloons arrive at the compound. Four of the gunmen head into the house, where they find Marley and Don Taylor in the kitchen. Taylor is hit five times and Marley once, a bullet passing through his chest and lodging in his left elbow. Rita, trying to escape with her children, is in her yellow Volkswagen when she is hit in the head. Friend Lewis Griffiths is also injured. Ambulances rush those injured to University College Hospital. Although this is never proven, it is believed that the assassination attempt was aimed at preventing Marley from performing at the "Smile Jamaica" concert in two days' time.

Um 21:30 Uhr findet ein Mordanschlag auf Marley statt, fünf bewaffnete Männer dringen in das Haus der Marleys an der 56 Hope Road in Kingston ein. Zwei weiße Datsun Saloons fahren vor dem Haus vor. Vier der fünf Bewaffneten dringen in das Haus ein, wo sie Marley und Don Taylor in der Küche vorfinden. Taylor wird fünfmal, Marley einmal getroffen, die Kugel geht durch seine Brust hindurch und bleibt in seinem Ellbogen stecken. Rita versucht mit den Kindern zu fliehen,

wird aber in ihrem gelben VW in den Kopf getroffen. Freund Lewis Griffiths wird ebenfalls verletzt. Die Verletzten werden umgehend von Krankenwagen ins University College Hospital geschafft. Es konnte zwar nie bewiesen werden, doch man nimmt an, dass Marley durch den Mordanschlag von der Teilnahme am zwei Tage später stattfindenden „Smile Jamaica"-Konzert abgehalten werden sollte.

Peu après 21h30, Marley est victime d'une tentative d'assassinat dans la maison qu'il partage avec Rita à Kingston. Deux berlines Datsun se garent devant le 56 Hope Road. Quatre des cinq hommes du commando se dirigent vers la maison, où ils trouvent Marley dans la cuisine avec Don Taylor. Cinq coups de feu atteignent Taylor et Marley est touché par une balle qui lui traverse le torse et se loge dans le coude gauche. Rita, qui tente de s'échapper avec ses enfants, est dans sa Volkswagen jaune lorsqu'elle est atteinte à la tête. Leur ami Lewis Griffiths est lui aussi blessé. Les ambulances arrivent sur le lieux et emportent les blessés à l'University College Hospital. Même si les preuves manquent, il semble que cette tentative d'assassinat visait à l'empêcher de chanter au concert « Smile Jamaica » prévu deux jours plus tard.

"When I decided to do this concert, there was no politics.
I just wanted to play for the love of the people."
„Als ich mich entschlossen habe, bei diesem Konzert zu spielen, hat Politik keine
Rolle gespielt. Ich wollte einfach nur aus Liebe zu den Leuten spielen."
« Quand j'ai décidé de faire ce concert, il n'y avait pas d'histoire de politique.
Je voulais juste jouer par amour pour les gens. »
BOB MARLEY, DECEMBER 5, 1976

SUNDAY, DECEMBER 5, 1976

Two days after the attempt on his life, Bob Marley performs in front of 80,000 fans at the "Smile Jamaica" concert, staged at the National Heroes Park in Kingston. Despite reservations, Marley opens with *War* and concludes the 15-song set by raising his shirt and showing his wounds.

Zwei Tage nach dem Attentat spielt Bob Marley vor 80.000 Fans beim „Smile Jamaica"-Konzert, das im National Heroes Park in Kingston stattfindet. Trotz aller Vorbehalte eröffnet Marley seine Setlist mit *War* und hebt nach den 15 Stücken sein Hemd und zeigt seine Wunden.

Deux jours après la tentative d'assassinat, Bob Marley se produit devant 80 000 personnes au National Heroes Park de Kingston, dans le cadre du concert « Smile Jamaica ». Malgré les réserves des organisateurs, Marley commence son tour de chant avec *War* et conclut ses quinze chansons en soulevant sa chemise pour montrer ses plaies.

JANUARY 1977

Having left Jamaica to convalesce in Nassau after the shooting, and then traveling to Miami, Delaware, and New York, Marley arrives in London with The Wailers to begin new recordings. During a prolific two-month period, they will cut enough material for two albums. With Al Anderson currently playing guitar for Peter Tosh, Junior Marvin steps in.

Marley hat Jamaika verlassen, um sich auf Nassau auszukurieren, fährt dann nach Miami, Delaware, und New York und trifft nun in London mit The Wailers zusammen, wo sie mit neuen Plattenaufnahmen beginnen. Im Laufe von zwei fruchtbaren Monaten spielen sie genug Material für zwei Alben ein. Al Anderson ist zu dem Zeitpunkt Gitarrist bei Peter Tosh und wird durch Junior Marvin ersetzt.

Marley quitte la Jamaïque pour aller se reposer à Nassau avant de partir pour Miami, le Delaware, puis New York. Il arrive à Londres avec les Wailers pour une nouvelle session d'enregistrement. En deux mois de travail prolifique, ils composent suffisamment de morceaux pour en faire deux albums. Al Anderson a remplacé Peter Tosh à la guitare et Junior Marvin a rejoint le groupe.

WEDNESDAY, APRIL 6, 1977

After being fined £50 for cannabis possession at Marylebone Magistrates Court in London, Marley tells awaiting reporters, "I smoke a joint of cannabis a day back home." The judge tells him to restrain himself while living in England. Aston Barrett is fined £25 on a similar charge.

Marley wird vor dem Marylebone Magistrates Court in London zu einer Strafe von 50 Pfund für Cannabisbesitz verurteilt. Den wartenden Reportern erzählt er: „Zu Hause rauche ich jeden Tag einen Joint." Der Richter ermahnt ihn, sich zusammenzureißen, solange er in England ist. Aston Barrett wird aus ähnlichen Gründen eine Geldstrafe von 25 Pfund aufgebrummt.

Marley est condamné à une amende de 50 livres pour possession de cannabis par le tribunal de Marylebone, à Londres, et déclare aux journalistes qui l'attendent : « Chez moi, je fume un joint de cannabis par jour. » Le juge lui demande de s'abstenir tant qu'il vit en Angleterre. Aston Barrett est condamné à une amende de 25 livres pour la même raison.

TUESDAY, MAY 10, 1977

The "Exodus" European tour begins at the Pavillon Baltard in Nogent-sur-Marne, Paris, France, ending with four dates at the Rainbow Theater in Finsbury Park, London, from June 1 to 4. The tour includes an appearance on BBC1 Television's "Top Of The Pops."

Die europäische „Exodus"-Tour beginnt im Pavillon Baltard in Nogent-sur-Marne, Paris, und endet mit vier Konzerten vom 1. bis 4. Juni im Rainbow Theater in Finsbury Park, London. Im Rahmen der Tournee findet auch ein Fernsehauftritt bei der BBC1-Sendung „Top Of The Pops" statt.

La tournée européenne « Exodus » commence au Pavillon Baltard, à Nogent-sur-Marne, près de Paris, et se termine par quatre concerts au Rainbow Theatre de Finsbury Park, à Londres, du 1ᵉʳ au 4 juin. Marley et les Wailers se produisent aussi dans la célèbre émission de la BBC1 « Top Of The Pops ».

"I am not a leader. Messenger. The words of the songs, not the person, is what attracts people."
„Ich bin kein Führer. Kein Prophet. Es sind die Texte der Lieder, von denen die Leute angezogen werden, nicht die Person."
« Je ne suis pas un guide. Messager. Ce sont les paroles des chansons et pas la personne, qui attirent les gens. »
BOB MARLEY, MELODY MAKER, MAY 21, 1977

"The turning point came halfway through with I Shot The Sheriff and War, in which Marley's fervent commitment to the exclusive religious and social concepts of Rastafarianism is most apparent."
„Der Wendepunkt kam mit den Songs I Shot The Sheriff und War, bei denen Marleys glühendes Engagement für die religiösen und sozialen Konzepte des Rastafari-Glaubens am deutlichsten werden."
« Le tournant est intervenu entre I Shot The Sheriff et War où l'engagement fervent de Marley dans la philosophie religieuse et sociale du mouvement rastafari est le plus flagrant. »
CLIVE BENNETT, THE TIMES, JUNE 5, 1977

"Bob doesn't have any feelings about politics."
„Bob hat keine politischen Überzeugungen."
« Bob n'a pas de sentiments à exprimer sur la politique. »
DON TAYLOR, MELODY MAKER, JUNE 1977

WEDNESDAY, JUNE 1 TO SATURDAY, JUNE 4, 1977

With the new album *Exodus* released on June 3 to rapturous reviews—it contains an equal blend of songs dealing with social injustice (with themes of Jah and Babylon at the fore) and more buoyant love songs—Marley and The Wailers play four career-defining performances at the Rainbow Theater in London. It will be the last time Neville Garrick's visual backdrop of Haile Selassie is used onstage. (In 2000, **The New York Times**, picking the video of the concert as one of the finest musical moments of the 20th Century, will place a copy in a time capsule to be opened in 3000.)

Das neue Album *Exodus* kommt am 3. Juni heraus und erntet überschwängliche Besprechungen – es enthält eine ausgewogene Mischung aus Titeln über soziale Ungerechtigkeit (mit besonderer Betonung der Themen Jah und Babylon) und lebhafteren Liebesliedern. Marley and The Wailers geben vier Konzerte im Rainbow Theater in London, die absolute Höhepunkte

ihrer Karriere darstellen. Es ist das letzte Mal, dass Neville Garricks Bild von Haile Selassie auf der Bühne als Hintergrund verwendet wird. (Im Jahr 2000 wählt die **New York Times** das Video des Konzerts als einen der größten musikalischen Augenblicke des 20. Jahrhunderts und steckt es in eine Zeitkapsel, die im Jahr 3000 geöffnet werden soll.)

Le 3 juin, la critique acclame la sortie de l'album *Exodus*, dont les titres alternent entre dénonciations de l'injustice sociale (en opposant Jah et Babylone) et chansons d'amour plus légères. Marley et les Wailers donnent quatre concerts exceptionnels au Rainbow Theatre de Londres. La toile de Neville Garrick représentant Hailé Sélassié est utilisée comme décor sur scène pour la dernière fois. (En 2000, le **New York Times** a choisi la vidéo d'un de ces concerts comme un des meilleurs moments de l'histoire de la musique au XXᵉ siècle, et l'a placée dans une capsule témoin qui sera ouverte en l'an 3000.)

THURSDAY, JULY 7, 1977
Marley is persuaded to visit a Harley Street consultant. His toe has been bandaged throughout most of the European tour, following a second soccer injury last month in France. He is diagnosed with melanoma, and doctors advise that his toe be amputated.

Marley wird überredet, einen Arzt an der Harley Street aufzusuchen. Seit einer neuerlichen Fußballverletzung im Vormonat in Frankreich ist sein Zeh während des Großteils der Europatournee verbunden gewesen. Bei ihm wird schwarzer Hautkrebs diagnostiziert, und die Ärzte empfehlen eine Amputation des Zehs.

Marley se laisse convaincre de consulter un médecin sur Harley Street. Il a gardé son orteil bandé pendant une grande partie de la tournée européenne après un deuxième accident de football en France, un mois plus tôt. Le médecin diagnostique un mélanome et lui conseille de se faire amputer l'orteil.

"Me toe can't cut off, you know. Me have to do something really wicked fe mek me toe cut off. It would be like ... you do something bad and you get beaten and you have to lose all you toe."
„Meinen Zeh kann man nicht einfach abschneiden. Da muss ich schon etwas sehr Schlimmes getan haben, dass man mir den Zeh abschneiden will. Das wäre wie ... man macht etwas ganz Schlimmes und man wird dafür bestraft und dafür muss man seinen Zeh hergeben."
« Mon orteil peut pas être coupé comme ça, mec. Il faudrait vraiment que je sois tordu pour me faire couper l'orteil. Ce serait comme si... tu fais quelque chose de mal, tu te fais battre, et après tu dois perdre tout l'orteil. »
BOB MARLEY, SOUNDS, MARCH 4, 1978

"We are Rasta.
Our struggle is for Africa."
„Wir sind Rasta.
Unser Kampf ist für Afrika."
« Nous sommes des rastas.
Nous nous battons pour l'Afrique. »
BOB MARLEY, THE TIMES, JUNE 1977

SUNDAY, AUGUST 7, 1977

Following an announcement that the rest of the "Exodus" tour is being cancelled, Marley has an operation performed by Dr. William Bacon at Cedars of Lebanon Hospital in Miami, Florida. A skin graft on a toe on his right foot removes a cancerous growth. The media is informed that he has injured his foot while playing his favorite game, soccer.

Der Rest der „Exodus"-Tournee wird abgesagt und Marley lässt sich von Dr. William Bacon im Cedars of Lebanon Hospital in Miami, Florida, operieren. An einem Zeh seines rechten Fußes wird ein Tumor entfernt und eine Hauttransplantation durchgeführt. Den Medien wird mitgeteilt, er habe sich bei seinem Lieblingssport Fußball den Fuß verletzt.

Le reste de la tournée « Exodus » est annulé et Marley se fait opérer par le Dr William Bacon à l'hôpital Cedars of Lebanon de Miami. Une excroissance cancéreuse est enlevée de son pied droit. La presse apprend qu'il s'est blessé en pratiquant son sport préféré, le football.

SATURDAY, FEBRUARY 25, 1978

Marley returns to Jamaica, following a 14-month self-imposed exile. His plane lands at Kingston's Norman Manley Airport and is greeted by a crowd of some 2,000 people. His return is ostensibly to give a benefit concert in aid of the truce that has been reached between rival political factions.

Nach einem vierzehnmonatigen, selbst auferlegten Exil kehrt Marley nach Jamaika zurück. Als sein Flugzeug auf dem Norman Manley Airport in Kingston landet, wird er von ca. 2.000 Menschen begrüßt. Anlass für seine Rückkehr ist ein Benefizkonzert zugunsten der Waffenruhe zwischen rivalisierenden politischen Fraktionen.

Marley retourne en Jamaïque, après 14 mois d'exil volontaire. Son avion atterrit à l'aéroport Norman Manley de Kingston, où il est accueilli par une foule de quelque 2 000 personnes. Il retrouve son île natale pour un concert destiné à soutenir la trêve à laquelle les factions politiques rivales jamaïcaines sont finalement parvenues.

SATURDAY, APRIL 22, 1978

The group headlines the "One Love Peace Concert" at the National Stadium in Kingston before a crowd of 30,000 people. Top local reggae acts, including Dennis Brown, Culture, Inner Circle, The Mighty Diamonds, a now solo (and openly spliff-smoking) Peter Tosh, and others, perform all day long. On stage, Marley unites Prime Minister Michael Manley and his opponent, Edward Seaga, in avowals of unity and common purpose. The concert ends well past midnight—12 years to the day since Haile Selassie's visit to the country—with two of Marley's sons onstage to dance to *Jah Love*.

Der Auftritt von Marley and The Wailers ist der wichtigste Act beim „One Love Peace Concert" im Nationalstadion in Kingston. Vor 30.000 Zuschauern spielen den ganzen Tag lang die größten lokalen Reggae-Künstler, darunter Dennis Brown, Culture, Inner Circle, die Mighty Diamonds und der auf offener Bühne kiffende Peter Tosh (jetzt Solo). Bob Marley bringt auf der Bühne Premierminister Michael Manley

und seinen Widersacher Edward Seaga unter Beschwörungen von Einheit und gemeinsamen Zielen zusammen. Das Konzert endet lange nach Mitternacht – auf den Tag genau zwölf Jahre nach Haile Selassies Besuch in Jamaika – mit *Jah Love*, wozu Marley und zwei seiner Söhne auf der Bühne tanzen.

Le groupe occupe la tête d'affiche du concert «One Love Peace» au National Stadium de Kingston, qui rassemble plus de 30 000 spectateurs. Les principaux artistes de reggae locaux sont présents, parmi lesquels Dennis Brown, Culture, Inner Circle, les Mighty Diamonds, Peter Tosh (désormais en solo, et consommateur ostensible de marijuana). Sur scène, Marley réunit le Premier ministre Michael Manley et son adversaire, Edward Seaga, qui témoignent de leur unité pour le bien commun. Le concert se termine bien après minuit – 12 ans jour pour jour après la visite d'Hailé Sélassié dans le pays – après que deux des fils de Marley l'ont rejoint sur scène pour danser sur *Jah Love*.

"His Imperial Majesty Haile Selassie I, run lightning, leading the people of the slaves to shake hands ... to show the people that everything is all right. Watch, watch, watch what you're doing, because I'm not so good at talking, but I hope you understand what I'm trying to say ... we've got to unite! The moon is high over my head, and I give my love instead ..."

„Seine Majestät, Kaiser Haile Selassie I., kam herab wie ein Blitz und führte die Völker der Sklaven, damit sie sich die Hand reichen ... und zeigte den Menschen, dass alles gut wird. Gebt acht, acht, acht, was ihr tut, das Reden liegt mir nicht so sehr, aber ich hoffe, ihr versteht, was ich sagen will ... Wir brauchen Einheit! Der Mond steht hoch über meinem Kopf und ich gebe meine Liebe ... "

« Sa Majesté Impériale Hailé Sélassié Ier, éclair de vie, engage les enfants d'esclaves à se serrer la main... pour montrer aux gens que tout va bien. Regardez, regardez, regardez ce que vous faites, parce que je ne suis pas très bon pour parler, mais j'espère que vous comprenez ce que j'essaie de dire... Il faut qu'on s'unisse! La lune au-dessus de ma tête, elle rayonne, et c'est mon amour que je donne... »

BOB MARLEY

*"It's a good heart this thing come out of. A good heart.
It couldn't come of politics."*
*„Diese Sache kommt aus einem guten Herzen. Einem guten
Herzen. Aus der Politik kann so etwas nicht kommen."*
*« C'est d'un cœur généreux que c'est sorti. D'un cœur bon.
Ça ne pouvait pas venir de la politique. »*
BOB MARLEY TO NEIL SPENCER, NME, APRIL 21, 1978

THURSDAY, MAY 18, 1978

Following the cancellation of the tour's first six dates, the "Kaya" tour gets underway at the Hill Auditorium in Ann Arbor, Michigan. Its North American leg will wind down on June 18 with a concert at the Music Inn in Lenox, Massachusetts.

Nach Absage der ersten sechs Termine geht die „Kaya"-Tour nun im Hill Auditorium in Ann Arbor, Michigan, los. Der letzte Gig in Nordamerika findet am 18. Juni im Music Inn in Lenox, Massachusetts, statt.

Les six premières dates de la tournée « Kaya » sont annulées, et les concerts commencent au Hill Auditorium d'Ann Arbor (Michigan). Le groupe quitte les États-Unis après une dernière date, le 18 juin, au Music Inn de Lenox (Massachusetts).

THURSDAY, JUNE 15, 1978
Senegal's Mohammadu Johnny Sekka, representing the combined African delegation of the United Nations, presents Marley with the Third World Peace Medal "on behalf of 500 million Africans" for his work for "equal rights and justice."

Der senegalesische Schauspieler Johnny Sekka überreicht Marley im Namen der afrikanischen Delegation der Vereinten Nationen die Friedensmedaille der Dritten Welt „stellvertretend für 500 Millionen Afrikaner" in Anerkennung seiner Bemühungen um „Gleichberechtigung und Gerechtigkeit".

L'acteur sénégalais Johnny Sekka, qui représente la délégation panafricaine des Nations unies, décerne à Marley la médaille de la Paix dans le tiers-monde « au nom de 500 millions d'Africains » pour saluer son travail en faveur « de l'égalité des droits et de la justice ».

"When you fight the revolution, you use guns ... Well music is the biggest gun, because it save. It no kill, right?"
„Wenn man Revolution machen will, braucht man Waffen ... Musik ist die wichtigste Waffe, weil sie Leben rettet. Damit bringt man niemanden um, oder?"
« Lorsqu'on fait la révolution, on utilise des armes... Eh bien, la musique est l'arme la plus puissante, parce qu'elle sauve. Elle tue pas, d'accord ? »
BOB MARLEY, JUNE 15, 1978

THURSDAY, JUNE 22, 1978

The group begins the European leg of the "Kaya" tour at the New Bingley Hall in Stafford, Staffordshire. After another 10 dates—including an appearance at the Roskilde Festival in Denmark—the trek will come to an end at the Forest National in Brussels, Belgium, on July 9. Four days later the group will once again appear on "Top Of The Pops," this time performing *Satisfy My Soul*.

Die „Kaya"-Europatournee beginnt in der New Bingley Hall in Stafford, England. Die Tour geht nach zehn weiteren Auftritten - unter anderem auch beim Roskilde Festival in Dänemark - im Forest National in Brüssel am 9. Juli zu Ende. Vier Tage später ist die Band noch einmal bei „Top Of The Pops" zu sehen, dieses Mal mit *Satisfy My Soul*.

Le groupe entame la partie européenne de la tournée « Kaya » au New Bingley Hall de Stafford (Staffordshire). Après dix autres dates - dont un concert au Roskilde Festival, au Danemark -, le périple s'achève au Forest National, à Bruxelles, le 9 juillet. Quatre jours plus tard, le groupe participe à l'émission « Top Of The Pops », cette fois avec *Satisfy My Soul*.

FRIDAY, JULY 14, 1978

Another North American leg of the "Kaya" tour begins at the Queen Elizabeth Theater in Vancouver, British Columbia. It will continue through August 5, when it will close at the Jai Alai Fronton in Miami, Florida. During a July 24 show at the Starlight Bowl in Burbank, California, Peter Tosh will join Marley onstage—the only time the two of them will appear together outside Jamaica since Tosh left the band.

Die „Kaya"-Tour führt die Band nach Nordamerika zurück, das erste Konzert findet im Queen Elizabeth Theater in Vancouver, Kanada, statt. Die Tour geht bis zum 5. August weiter, das letzte Konzert ereignet sich im Jai Alai Fronton in Miami, Florida. Beim Auftritt am 24. Juli im Starlight Bowl in Burbank, Kalifornien,

kommt Peter Tosh zu Marley auf die Bühne – es ist das einzige Mal, dass die beiden außerhalb Jamaikas zusammen auftreten, seit Peter Tosh die Band verlassen hat.

Le groupe retourne en Amérique du Nord pour achever la tournée « Kaya ». Il se produit d'abord au Queen Elizabeth Theater de Vancouver (Colombie-Britannique) et termine sa tournée le 5 août au Jai Alai Fronton de Miami. Pendant le concert du 24 juillet au Starlight Bowl de Burbank (Californie), Peter Tosh rejoint Marley sur scène – c'est la première et la dernière fois que les deux hommes se produisent ensemble en dehors de la Jamaïque depuis que Tosh a quitté le groupe.

AFRICA UNITE

A PEOPLE WITHOUT THE KNOWLEDGE OF THEIR PAST HISTORY, ORIGIN
IS LIKE A TREE WITHOUT ROOTS

DECEMBER 1978
Marley makes a short trip, his first, to Kenya and his avowed spiritual home, Ethiopia. While there, he attends a rally calling for independence in Rhodesia.

Marley unternimmt seine erste Afrikareise, einen kurzen Trip nach Kenia und in seine spirituelle Wahl-heimat Äthiopien. Dort nimmt er an einer Kundgebung für die Unabhängigkeit Rhodesiens teil.

Marley effectue son premier voyage en Afrique : il se rend au Kenya, puis sur sa terre spirituelle d'adop-tion, l'Éthiopie. Il y assiste à un meeting pour l'indépen-dance de la Rhodésie.

FEBRUARY 1979

Marley and The Wailers return to the studio—this time their own Tuff Gong facility—to begin work on new material that will emerge as *Survival*. Tuff Gong also opens up its own pressing plant.

Marley and The Wailers kehren ins Plattenstudio zurück – dieses Mal ihr eigenes Tuff Gong Studio – und beginnen mit den Aufnahmen von neuem Material, aus dem dann *Survival* entsteht. Tuff Gong eröffnet auch ein eigenes Presswerk.

Marley et les Wailers retournent en studio - cette fois dans leurs locaux de Tuff Gong - pour travailler sur les chansons qui donneront corps à l'album *Survival*. Tuff Gong ouvre aussi sa propre usine de pressage de vinyles.

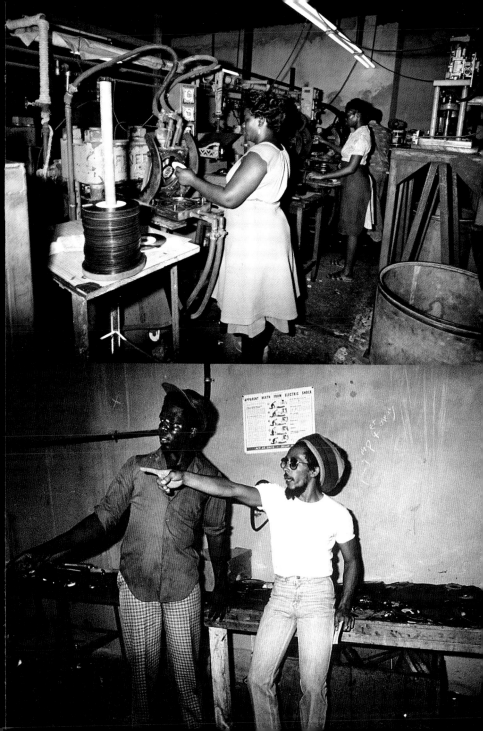

THURSDAY, APRIL 5, 1979
The "Babylon By Bus" tour—the group's only visit to Oceania—begins at the Shinjuku Kosei Nenkin Kaikan in Shinjuku, Tokyo, Japan. Other Japanese dates will follow before a sole concert in New Zealand, eight in Australia, and two in Hawaii. The tour will end on May 6 at the Waikiki Shell in Honolulu.

Die Tournee „Babylon By Bus", einziger Abstecher der Band nach Ozeanien, beginnt im Shinjuku Kosei Nenkin Kaikan in Shinjuku, Tokio, Japan. Auf dem Kalender stehen weitere Termine in Japan, ein einziges Konzert in Neuseeland, acht in Australien und zwei in Hawaii. Die Tour endet am 6. Mai im Waikiki Shell in Honolulu.

La tournée « Babylon By Bus » - qui emmène le groupe en Océanie pour la première et dernière fois - démarre au Kosei Nenkin Kaikan de Shinjuku, près de Tokyo, et se poursuit quelques jours au Japon avant de gagner la Nouvelle-Zélande pour un concert unique, puis l'Australie pour huit dates et Hawaï pour deux concerts. Elle se termine le 6 mai au Waikiki Shell d'Honolulu.

SATURDAY, JULY 7, 1979
Marley takes part in "Reggae Sunsplash II," staged at Jarrett Park in Montego Bay, Jamaica. It is his first performance on Jamaican soil since the "One Love Peace Concert"—and will prove to be his last.

Marley nimmt an dem Festival „Reggae Sunsplash II" teil, das im Jarrett Park in Montego Bay, Jamaika, stattfindet. Es ist sein erster Auftritt in Jamaika seit dem „One Love Peace Concert" - und es wird auch sein letzter sein.

Marley participe au festival « Reggae Sunsplash II », organisé au Jarrett Park, à Montego Bay, sur son île natale. C'est sa première performance en public sur le sol jamaïcain depuis le concert « One Love Peace ». Ce sera la dernière.

SATURDAY, JULY 21, 1979

Marley and The Wailers top the bill at the "Amandla Festival Of Unity" concert—a benefit for Relief and Humanitarian Aid in Southern Africa at Harvard Stadium in Cambridge, Massachusetts. Also on the bill are Patti LaBelle, Eddie Palmieri, Olatunji Jabula, and special guest Dick Gregory.

Marley and The Wailers spielen als Höhepunkt des „Amandla Festival Of Unity" – ein Benefizkonzert zugunsten humanitärer Hilfe für Südafrika im Harvard Stadium in Cambridge, Massachusetts. Außer ihnen nehmen Patti LaBelle, Eddie Palmieri, Olatunji Jabula und Special Guest Dick Gregory teil.

Marley et les Wailers sont acclamés à l'Amandla Festival Of Unity – un concert de charité organisé pour financer l'envoi d'une aide humanitaire d'urgence pour l'Afrique du Sud – au Harvard Stadium de Cambridge (Massachusetts). Ils partagent l'affiche avec Patti LaBelle, Eddie Palmieri, Olatunji Jabula et Dick Gregory.

MONDAY, SEPTEMBER 24, 1979

The group performs at a benefit concert for Rastafarian children at the National Heroes Stadium in Kingston.

Die Band spielt bei einem Benefizkonzert für Rastafari-Kinder im National Heroes Stadium in Kingston.

Le groupe participe à un concert de charité pour les enfants du mouvement rastafari au National Heroes Stadium de Kingston.

"A young man who understands racism, who understands poverty,
who understands all the hurts, and he didn't let it defeat him. He set out
to share his joy, his love, his great respect, his religion, his spiritual
power with the whole world."

„Ein junger Mann, der weiß, was Rassismus ist, der weiß, was Armut ist,
der alle Demütigungen kennengelernt hat und sich von nichts hat
unterkriegen lassen. Er hat es sich zum Ziel gesetzt, seine Lebensfreude,
seine Liebe, seinen großen Respekt, seine Religion und seine spirituelle
Kraft mit der ganzen Welt zu teilen."

« Un jeune homme qui comprend le racisme, qui comprend la pauvreté,
qui comprend toutes les douleurs et qui ne les a pas laissées le vaincre.
Il a décidé de partager sa joie, son amour, son grand respect, sa religion
et son pouvoir spirituel avec le monde entier. »

DICK GREGORY

THURSDAY, OCTOBER 25 TO SUNDAY
OCTOBER 28, 1979

At the start of a North American tour that will see the band play 47 shows in 49 days, The Wailers perform at the legendary Apollo Theater in Harlem, New York. Shortly after the concerts, Marley tells Carol Cooper of **The Village Voice**: "We don't have anything against the white man in the sense of color prejudice, but black is right."

Zum Auftakt der Nordamerikatournee, bei der die Band 47 Konzerte an 49 Tagen gibt, spielen The Wailers im legendären Apollo Theater in Harlem, New York. Kurz nach den Apollo-Konzerten sagt Marley zu Carol Cooper von der Zeitung **The Village Voice**: „Wir haben nichts gegen Weiße, im Sinne von Vorurteilen gegen ihre Hautfarbe, aber schwarz ist richtig."

À l'aube d'une nouvelle tournée américaine qui comptera 47 concerts en 49 jours, les Wailers se produisent au légendaire Apollo Theater de Harlem, à New York. Peu après les concerts à l'Apollo, Marley déclare à Carol Cooper, de l'hebdomadaire **The Village Voice** : « Nous n'avons rien contre l'homme blanc, nous n'avons pas de préjugés sur la couleur, mais le noir, c'est bien. »

"It's a long way from the sharp-strutting, jive-talkin', coke-sniffin', git-down paaarrty world of popular black American idealization to the resolute Rastafarian idealism."

„Es ist ein langer Weg vom schwarzamerikanischen Ideal der todschicken, coole Sprüche schwingenden, Kokain schniefenden supersexy Partyszene zum resoluten Idealismus der Rastafaris."

« Il y a une grande différence entre l'idéalisation du monde mise en scène par les Noirs américains – frime, sapes, baratin, sniffage de coke et "vas-y bébé bouge ton corps" – et l'idéalisme résolu des rastas. »

NEIL SPENCER, NME

WEDNESDAY, NOVEMBER 7, 1979
Stevie Wonder joins Marley onstage at the Penn
Hall in Philadelphia, at a benefit concert for the Black
Music Association. They sing *Get Up, Stand Up* and
Exodus together.

Stevie Wonder kommt in der Penn Hall in Philadelphia bei einem Benefizkonzert für die Black Music
Association zu Marley auf die Bühne. Sie singen
zusammen *Get Up, Stand Up* und *Exodus*.

Stevie Wonder rejoint Marley sur scène au Penn
Hall de Philadelphie, lors d'un concert de charité au
profit de la Black Music Association. Ils chantent
ensemble *Get Up, Stand Up* et *Exodus*.

"I know that this is the music that His Majesty is well pleased of, because He loves music,
let's face it ... 'Cause God listens to music ... if you're singing, God's listening."
„Ich weiß, dass Seine Majestät sehr zufrieden mit dieser Musik ist, weil er Musik liebt,
das ist ja wohl klar ... Gott hört Musik ... wenn du singst, dann hört Gott dir zu."
« Je sais que c'est la musique qui réjouit sa Majesté, parce qu'Il aime la musique,
il faut le savoir... Parce que Dieu écoute la musique... Si tu chantes, Dieu t'écoute. »
BOB MARLEY, NOVEMBER 1979

THE 1980^S

DIE 1980ER

LES ANNÉES 1980

FRIDAY, JANUARY 4 & SATURDAY, JANUARY 5, 1980

Marley and The Wailers perform at the Gymnase Omnisport Bongo in Libreville, Gabon, to celebrate President Omar Bongo's 45th birthday. Shortly thereafter, Marley fires Taylor as his manager, alleging that he underpaid the band for these two concerts.

Marley and The Wailers spielen im Gymnase Omnisport Bongo in Libreville, Gabun, zur Feier von Präsident Omar Bongos 45. Geburtstag. Kurz danach feuert Marley seinen Manager Taylor, weil er der Band angeblich für die beiden Konzerte zu wenig ausbezahlt hat.

Marley et les Wailers se produisent au Gymnase Omnisport Bongo de Libreville, au Gabon, pour célébrer le 45ᵉ anniversaire du Président Omar Bongo. Peu après, Marley renvoie Taylor, qu'il accuse de les avoir sous-payés pour ces deux concerts.

MARCH 1980

Marley and The Wailers help Chris Blackwell celebrate the opening of Island Records' Brazilian office in Rio de Janeiro. While there, Marley plays soccer with Brazilian soccer legend Paulo César.

Marley and The Wailers feiern zusammen mit Chris Blackwell die Eröffnung der brasilianischen Niederlassung von Island Records in Rio de Janeiro. Marley spielt Fußball mit der brasilianischen Kickerlegende Paulo César.

Marley et les Wailers aident Chris Blackwell à fêter l'ouverture du bureau brésilien d'Island Records à Rio de Janeiro. Pendant ce séjour, Marley joue au football avec la légende locale Paulo César.

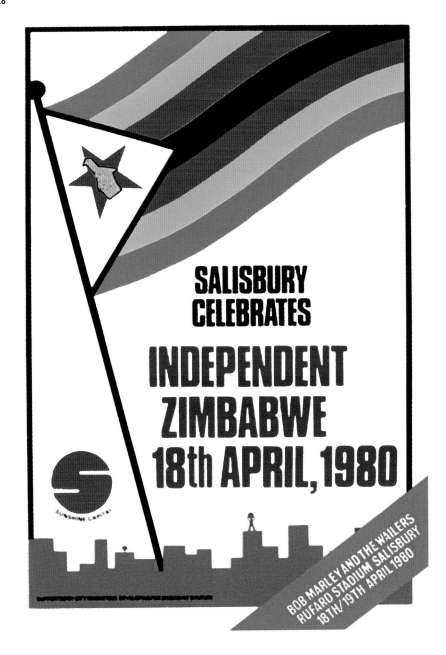

FRIDAY, APRIL 18 & SATURDAY, APRIL 19, 1980

Marley and The Wailers appear at the Independence Day celebrations at The Rufaro Stadium in Harare, Zimbabwe, in front of HRH Prince Charles and President Robert Mugabe. Prince Charles ceremoniously hands over the lowered Union Jack flag to Lord Christopher Soames, the outgoing Governor of Southern Rhodesia. The first concert is interrupted by drifting tear gas outside the stadium. The band underwrites the entire cost of the trip.

Marley and The Wailers treten bei der Unabhängigkeitsfeier Simbabwes im Rufaro Stadium in Harare vor Prinz Charles und Präsident Robert Mugabe auf. Prinz Charles überreicht Lord Christopher Soames, dem scheidenden Gouverneur von Südrhodesien, die abgenommene britische Flagge. Das erste Konzert wird von Tränengas unterbrochen, das von der Straße ins Stadion hereinzieht. Die Band kommt für alle mit dieser Reise verbundenen Kosten selbst auf.

Marley et les Wailers participent aux célébrations de l'indépendance du Zimbabwe au stade Rufaro d'Harare, en présence de SAR le prince Charles et du président Robert Mugabe. Le premier concert est interrompu en raison de jets de gaz lacrymogène à l'extérieur du stade. Le prince Charles remet cérémonieusement le drapeau plié de l'Union Jack à Lord Christopher Soames, le gouverneur sortant de la Rhodésie du Sud. Le groupe a pris en charge la totalité du coût du voyage.

*"And we feel good feh taste little tear gas
in Zimbabwe, get a little o' th' oppression there."*
*„Und wir sind froh, dass wir ein bisschen
was vom Tränengas in Simbabwe mitgekriegt haben,
bisschen was von der Unterdrückung da."*
*« Et ça nous a fait du bien de sentir un peu
de gaz lacrymo au Zimbabwe, d'avoir un aperçu
de l'oppression qui sévit là-bas. »*
BOB MARLEY, SMASH HITS, AUGUST 7, 1980

122

FRIDAY, MAY 30, 1980

Promoting the album of the same name, the "Uprising" tour kicks off at the Hallenstadion in Zurich, Switzerland. It will take the group through Germany, France, England, Norway, Sweden, Denmark, Belgium, the Netherlands, Italy—including a date at the San Siro Stadium attended by more than 100,000 people—Spain, Ireland, Scotland, and Wales before coming to an end at the New Bingley Hall in Stafford, Staffordshire on July 13. *Uprising* will prove to be the last album released in Marley's lifetime; it includes the pop gem *Could You Be Loved* and the timeless, solo acoustic classic *Redemption Song*.

Die „Uprising"-Tour für das neue Album gleichen Namens geht im Hallenstadion in Zürich los. Die Band tourt durch Deutschland, Frankreich, England, Norwegen, Schweden, Dänemark, Belgien, die Niederlande, Italien – mit einem Konzert im Mailänder San Siro Stadion vor über 100.000 Zuschauern – Spanien, Irland, Schottland und Wales, bevor die Reise in der New Bingley Hall in Stafford, Staffordshire am 13. Juli zu Ende geht. *Uprising* wird das letzte Album bleiben, das zu Marleys Lebzeiten veröffentlicht wird; es enthält die Pophymne *Could You Be Loved* und den zeitlosen Soloklassiker *Redemption Song*.

La tournée « Uprising » montée pour promouvoir le nouvel album, est lancée au Hallenstadion de Zurich, en Suisse. Elle emmènera le groupe en Allemagne, en France, en Angleterre, en Norvège, en Suède, au Danemark, en Belgique, aux Pays-Bas, en Italie – notamment pour une date au stade San Siro de Milan

devant 100 000 personnes – en Espagne, en Irlande, en Écosse et au Pays de Galles, pour s'achever au New Bingley Hall de Stafford (Staffordshire) le 13 juillet. *Uprising* sera le dernier album édité du vivant de Marley ; il inclut le bijou pop *Could You Be Loved* et l'éternel classique acoustique *Redemption Song*.

SATURDAY, JUNE 7, 1980

The group headlines the "Summer Of '80 Garden Party" at the Crystal Palace Bowl in South London, supported by The Average White Band, The Q-Tips, and special guest Joe Jackson.

Marley and The Wailerst sind der Hauptact bei der „Summer Of '80 Garden Party" in der Crystal Palace Bowl in South London, Vorgruppen sind Average White Band und die Q-Tips, Special Guest ist Joe Jackson.

Le groupe est à l'affiche de la garden-party «Summer Of '80» au Crystal Palace Bowl, dans le sud de Londres, avec l'Average White Band, les Q-Tips, et Joe Jackson comme invité spécial.

SUNDAY, SEPTEMBER 21, 1980

Having performed a pair of concerts with co-headliners The Commodores at Madison Square Garden on Friday and Saturday, following the opening of a United States tour in Boston, Massachusetts, on the 16th, Marley collapses while jogging with his friends Danny Sims and Alan "Skill" Cole in Central Park, New York.

Nachdem er am Freitag und Samstag zwei Konzerte im Madison Square Garden in New York gegeben hat, bei denen auch die Commodores spielten, bricht Marley beim Joggen im Central Park zusammen, seine Freunde Danny Sims und Alan „Skill" Cole sind bei ihm; die neue Amerikatournee hatte erst am 16. September in Boston, Massachusetts, begonnen.

La tournée américaine a commencé à Boston (Massachusetts) le 16 septembre. Après deux concerts avec les Commodores au Madison Square Garden de New York le vendredi et le samedi, Marley s'effondre alors qu'il court dans Central Park avec ses amis Danny Sims et Alan « Skill » Cole.

TUESDAY, SEPTEMBER 23, 1980

Marley makes his last live appearance at the Stanley Theater in Pittsburgh, Pennsylvania. Shortly afterwards he is flown to New York and admitted to Sloan-Kettering Hospital. He is diagnosed as having a brain tumor and given one month to live. The remainder of the tour is cancelled.

Marleys letzter Live-Auftritt im Stanley Theater in Pittsburgh, Pennsylvania. Direkt danach wird er nach New York ins Sloan-Kettering Hospital geflogen. Dort wird ein Gehirntumor diagnostiziert, seine Lebenserwartung wird auf einen Monat beziffert. Die restliche Tournee wird abgesagt.

Marley se produit pour la dernière fois en public au Stanley Theater de Pittsburgh (Pennsylvanie). Peu après, il est embarqué à bord d'un avion pour New York et admis à l'hôpital Sloan-Kettering. Les médecins diagnostiquent une tumeur au cerveau et lui donnent un mois à vivre. Le reste de la tournée est annulé.

SATURDAY, OCTOBER 4, 1980

Stevie Wonder's *Master Blaster (Jammin')*, inspired by Marley, hits number 2 in the United Kingdom. It will peak at number 4 on the United States chart in December.

Stevie Wonders *Master Blaster (Jammin')*, inspiriert von Marley, schafft es in den englischen Charts auf den 2. Platz. In den US-Charts erreicht der Song im Dezember Platz 4.

Master Blaster (Jammin'), la chanson de Stevie Wonder inspirée de Marley, atteint la deuxième place des ventes au Royaume-Uni. Elle se hissera à la quatrième place du classement américain en décembre.

TUESDAY, OCTOBER 7, 1980

Doctors at the Memorial Sloan-Kettering Cancer Center inform Marley that the cancer has spread from his brain to his lungs and stomach. He begins a series of radiation treatments and chemotherapy.

Die Ärzte im Memorial Sloan-Kettering Cancer Center informieren Marley, dass der Krebs sich bereits vom Gehirn auf Lunge und Magen ausgebreitet hat. Er beginnt mit Strahlenbehandlung und Chemotherapie.

Les médecins du Centre de cancérologie de Sloan-Kettering informent Marley que le cancer s'est étendu aux poumons et à l'estomac. Il commence une série de rayons et de séances de chimiothérapie.

"One God, One Aim, One Destiny, and that will overcome all things. Personally, see, if them no deal with Rastafari, me no see the solution. Love, love is the answer. You see, love. Love is God. That is the solution for what going on. Only God can solve it."

„Ein Gott, Ein Ziel, Ein Schicksal, und das wird alles überwinden. Ich persönlich, ich glaube nicht, dass es eine Lösung gibt, wenn man sich nicht Rastafari anvertraut. Liebe, Liebe ist die Antwort. Liebe, verstehst du. Liebe ist Gott. Das ist die Lösung für alles, was hier vor sich geht. Nur Gott kann das lösen."

« Un seul Dieu, Un seul But, Un seul Destin, c'est ce qui compte plus que tout. Personnellement, tu vois, s'ils ne se rapprochent pas du rastafari, je ne vois pas la solution. L'amour, l'amour est la réponse. Tu vois, l'amour. L'amour est Dieu. C'est ça la solution à tout ce qui se passe. Seul Dieu peut le résoudre. »

BOB MARLEY

TUESDAY, NOVEMBER 4, 1980
Marley is baptized by the Archbishop of the Christian Ethiopian Orthodox Church in Kingston, converting to Christian Rastafarianism and taking the new name Berhane Selassie ("Light Of The Holy Trinity").

Marley wird vom Erzbischof der christlichen äthiopisch-orthodoxen Kirche in Kingston getauft, tritt damit offiziell zum christlichen Rastafarianismus über und nimmt den neuen Namen Berhane Selassie an („Licht der heiligen Dreifaltigkeit").

Marley est baptisé par l'archevêque de l'Église orthodoxe chrétienne d'Éthiopie à Kingston ; il se convertit ainsi au christianisme rasta et prend le nom de Berhane Sélassié (« Lumière de la Sainte Trinité »).

SUNDAY, NOVEMBER 9, 1980
On the advice of a friend, Jamaican doctor Carlton Frazier, Marley flies to controversial cancer specialist Dr. Josef Issels at his cancer treatment center in Rottach-Egern, Bavaria, West Germany, for treatment.

Auf Anraten eines Freundes, des jamaikanischen Arztes Carlton Frazier, fliegt Marley zu dem umstrittenen Krebsspezialisten Dr. Josef Issels in Rottach-Egern in Bayern und lässt sich in dessen Privatklinik behandeln.

Sur le conseil d'un ami, le médecin jamaïcain Carlton Frazier, Marley s'envole pour consulter le cancérologue controversé Josef Issels dans sa clinique privée de Rottach-Egern, en Bavière (Allemagne).

FRIDAY, FEBRUARY 6, 1981
Marley's family and The Wailers celebrate his birthday in Germany. Marley's mother wants him to come
home; Issels advises against it.

Marleys Familie und The Wailers feiern seinen
Geburtstag mit ihm in Deutschland. Marleys Mutter
will, dass er heimkehrt, Dr. Issels rät ihm davon ab.

La famille de Marley et les Wailers célèbrent son
anniversaire en Allemagne. Sa mère veut qu'il rentre à
la maison ; le Dr Issels le lui déconseille.

FRIDAY, APRIL 17, 1981
Marley is awarded Jamaica's Order of Merit, the country's third-highest honor, given to an individual for exceptional work of international status. He is the sixth recipient of the award. Because he is still receiving treatment in Bavaria, Marley's award is accepted in his absence by his son Ziggy.

Marley wird der jamaikanische „Order of Merit" verliehen, die dritthöchste Auszeichnung des Landes, mit der herausragende Leistungen von internationalem Rang gewürdigt werden. Er ist der sechste Empfänger der Auszeichnung. Da er nach wie vor in Bayern behandelt wird, nimmt Marleys Sohn Ziggy den Orden in seiner Abwesenheit entgegen.

Marley reçoit la médaille jamaïcaine de l'Ordre du Mérite, la troisième distinction la plus importante de l'île, qui salue le travail exceptionnel d'un individu ayant acquis une stature internationale. Il est la sixième personne à en être honorée. Marley est toujours en traitement en Bavière et c'est son fils Ziggy qui reçoit la médaille en son nom.

MONDAY, MAY 11, 1981
Two days after flying back to Miami, Marley dies at approximately 11:30 A.M. at Cedars of Lebanon Hospital. His mother, Cedella Booker, and lawyer Diane Jobson are present when he passes away. He is 36. He leaves behind 11 children and an estate currently valued at $30 million.

Zwei Tage nach dem Rückflug nach Miami stirbt Marley um ca. 11:30 Uhr im Cedars of Lebanon Hospital. Bei seinem Tod sind seine Mutter Cedella Booker und seine Anwältin Diane Jobson bei ihm. Er ist 36 Jahre alt. Er hinterlässt 11 Kinder und einen auf 30 Mio. Dollar geschätzten Nachlass.

Deux jours après son retour à Miami, Marley rend son dernier souffle aux environs de 11h30 à l'hôpital Cedars of Lebanon. Sa mère, Cedella Booker, et son avocate Diane Jobson sont présentes au moment de sa mort. Il a 36 ans et laisse derrière lui 11 enfants et une fortune estimée à 30 millions de dollars.

"The lines of people queuing extended in serpentine pleats the length of the building, and every so often there'd be a scampering and a scurrying as the lines fragmented; then the police ran in spraying tear gas, and little youths, all ready in their running shoes; shrunken grannies; country dreads with their shorn-off trousers frayed below the knee; Twelve Tribes dreads with handsome red, green, and gold tams; turbaned African daughters; groups of cornrowed schoolgirls, all pell-melled away from the police advance."

„Eine ewig lange Kette von Menschen schlängelte sich an dem Gebäude entlang und war in ständiger Bewegung, bis die Kette zerbrach, weil die Polizei anrückte und Tränengas sprühte. Kleine Jungen standen in ihren Turnschuhen bereit, hutzelige alte Mütterchen, Dreads vom Lande mit abgeschnittenen, ausgefransten Hosen, Mitglieder der Twelve Tribes mit prächtigen rot-grüngoldenen Rasta-Mützen, Töchter Afrikas mit Turban, Gruppen von Schulmädchen mit Flechtfrisuren, alle rannten Hals über Kopf vor der anrückenden Polizei davon."

« La file des admirateurs qui attendaient pour l'approcher serpentait sur toute la longueur du bâtiment ; les gens se mettaient à trottiner à chaque fois que la file se rompait. La police s'est avancée en lançant des gaz lacrymogènes : les gamins en baskets prêts à déguerpir, les mamies courbées, les rastas de la campagne avec leurs pantalons usés jusqu'à la corde et déchirés sous les genoux, les « bobos dreads » des Douze Tribus coiffés de leur élégant bonnet rouge, vert et or, les filles africaines enturbannées, les groupes d'écolières aux cheveux tressés, tous s'éparpillèrent devant la charge. »

VIVIEN GOLDMAN, NME, MAY 30, 1981

WEDNESDAY, MAY 20 & THURSDAY, MAY 21, 1981
His body lies in state at the National Arena in Kingston. An estimated 500,000 people—half the island's population—show their respects.

Sein Leichnam wird in der National Arena in Kingston aufgebahrt. Geschätzte 500.000 Jamaikaner - die Hälfte der Inselbevölkerung - erweisen ihm die letzte Ehre.

La dépouille de Marley est exposée à la National Arena de Kingston. Quelque 500 000 personnes - la moitié de la population de l'île - viennent s'y recueillir.

BOB MARLEY DIES OF CANCER

The Reggae King was only 36

THE HON. ROBERT NESTA MARLEY (Bob) O.M., the most widely acclaimed Jamaican musician ever, died of cancer in the Cedars of Lebanon Hospital in Miami, Florida on Monday.

Bob Marley, as he was known worldwide, was on his way home to receive the honour of Order of Merit which was conferred on him by the Government less than a month ago. The reggae singer was the biggest selling recording artiste in the history of Jamaican music having sold well over 20 million records.

His battle with cancer started some eight months ago during his last concert tour of the United States. Marley had finished the European leg of his tour and was performing in Madison Square Gardens, New York, in October last, when he fainted. His connections reported that he was suffering from exhaustion. However, it was later revealed as cancer.

Marley who was 36 years old was returning home from Bavaria, West Germany, where he had undergone chemo-therapy treatment for the disease at the clinic of Dr. Josef Issels, whose unorthodox approach to the treatment of cancer has been scoffed at by leading European experts.

The singer had stopped off in Miami because daily treatment which was required for the disease was said to be probably non-existent in Jamaica. He arrived in Miami on Thursday and entered the hospital on Friday. On Monday he was in his room with his wife, Rita, his mother, Mrs. Cedella Booker and his attorney/ business agent and constant travelling companion, Miss Diane Jobson. He requested that his wife fetch something from his South Miami home where his mother resides, but he died before she returned.

DOCTORS GAVE UP

THE STORY OF HIS ILLNESS goes back to last October when he began treatment at the Sloan-Kettering Hospital in New York for the disease. After he was given up by the American doctors who gave him until Christmas to live, he went to Bavaria for treatment.

He stayed with Dr. Issels at Rottach-Egern near Lake Tegern in the Bavarian Alps. When he arrived there he was partly paralysed by a brain tumor. He had cancer in the stomach, his "locks" were shorn and he had a ban placed on his drinking alcohol or smoking. His mouth appeared twisted and he was weak after losing a great deal of weight.

However, in an exclusive interview with John Stevenson of Associated Newspapers, he said: "Like so many other patients who come here (Issel's place), I was given up by the doctors to die. Now I know I can live. I have proved it."

Marley was one of the world's most popular pop singers. He was also a very successful song writer, having written million selling hits for entertainers such as Johnny Nash and Eric Clapton. He was also a producer and businessman and owner of Tuff Gong Recording Studios on Hope Road, St. Andrew, one of the largest in the Caribbean.

BORN IN ST. ANN

HE WAS BORN IN RHODEN HALL, ST. ANN, on February 6, 1945. His father was a British Naval Captain, Norman Marley of Liverpool, England, who was in Jamaica during the Second World War. His mother, Cedella Booker, emigrated to the United States several years ago and now lives in Miami, Florida.

Bob, who became a welder, his mother and two brothers and a sister moved to Kingston when he was nine. They lived at Waltham Park Road and later at Wilton Gardens (Rema), Trench Town.

He started recording in 1963 and his first record was "Judge Not". Although he and his group, the Wailers, which included Peter McIntosh and Bunny Livingstone and which was formed in Wilton Gardens, made several hit songs including "Rude Boy Ska", "Simmer Down," "Stir It Up" and "Nice Time" during the '60s, they never achieved real success until the early '70s.

In 1972 the Wailers signed a contract with Island Records and the first album "Catch A Fire", which was distributed worldwide by Island was a moderate success. Island is owned by Jamaican businessman, Chris Blackwell, who also gave the start to the careers of other Jamaican entertainers such as Millie Small, Jimmy Cliff and Owen Gray.

After the initial success of "Catch A Fire" the group recorded "Burning", before they split. Bob then formed a band including his two main stay musicians, Aston "Family Man" Barrett on bass and Carlton Barrett on drums and the singing group, the I-Threes, comprising his wife Rita, a former lead singer of the Soulettes, Judy Mowatt formerly of the Gayletts and Marcia Griffiths.

Bob Marley and the Wailers went on to make the "Natty Dread" album, and then the "Rastaman Vibrations" album which became their first million seller. Since then, they have recorded several other albums including "Survival", "Kaya" and his latest "Uprising" which was released last summer.

NATIONAL HONOUR

IN APRIL THIS YEAR, BOB MARLEY was awarded the Nation's third highest honour, the Order of Merit (O.M.). Also in April, he was awarded a Certificate of Merit by the Gleaner Company for his contribution to entertainment.

In 1980 he was invited by the newly elected Patriotic Front Government of Zimbabwe to perform at celebrations marking Independence. In 1976 he was awarded the Deutsche Schallplatten Award by Ariola Records for sales of his records.

In 1978 he was the guest performer at the Peace Concert which was organized by the Peace Committee made up of several political gangs to try to end tribal political warfare in the Corporate Area.

IN THE EARLY YEARS Bob and the Wailers did several ballards including "It Hurts to Be Alone" and "I'm Still Waiting" as well as several Ska tunes dealing with life in general. The most popular among the latter were "Simmer Down", "Rude Boy Ska", "Dancing Shoes" and "Bend Down Low".

Tunes like "Rude Boy Ska" and Peter McIntosh's "I Am The Toughest" became anthems of the rebellious youth population of the 1960s, in a period when guns were becoming quite prevalent. Kingston was seething with rival gangs and political rivalry started to develop into bloody war. These songs made the Wailers the idols of those youths, but in later years the group was to become the conscience of the young with their strong Rastafarian influence and a rigid opposition to political division which they termed "tribalism".

By the early '70s they were singing tunes like "400 years", "Jah Live" and "Guava Jelly" which appealed largely to adults, while still dealing with the explosive issues of hunger and poverty.

His last local appearance was at the Reggae Sunsplash show in Montego Bay in July, 1979.

A RELIGIOUS MAN – MARLEY READING HIS BIBLE.

P.N.P. REGRETS HIS PASSING

The People's National Party in a release on the death of Bob Marley said that his loss was undoubtedly one of the saddest events of recent times.

The release said:

"The death of Jamaica's International star, Bob Marley, is undoubtedly one of the saddest events of recent times.

"When news of his illness began to be circulated some months ago, all Jamaica hoped and prayed that he would recover and be restored to good health. This was not to be. He will be sadly missed on the musical scene.

"In a comparatively few years this young man has earned the love, respect and honour of his country and has placed Jamaica and our music on the lips of millions of people in the continents and countries all over the globe. He was Ambassador Extraordinary of his country and people.

"His dedication to the music he helped to create and publicise and the excellence of his presentations during these years have earned him an honoured place among musicians of the world. But Marley was not just a musician; he had the rare gift that made him at once a brilliant performer and song-writer, but above all he was a champion and an apostle of justice. The plight of oppressed people all over the world, especially the black race; their struggles over the centuries for dignity and self-expression; their hopes and aspirations and protest found voice in his music which commented on past and present events and prophesied of things to come. It would do our country well at this time to listen to the many messages he articulated.

"Perhaps Bob Marley was just 'fulfilling the Book' which was the code of his religious beliefs. But the musical heritage he left us is one of the treasures of this nation, and his place in Jamaica's history is well assured by this. May he find the peace he so often invoked for his people.

"On behalf of the People's National Party I wish to extend our profound sympathy to his wife Rita, his children, his relatives and his brothers."

ALL FOR PEACE: Marley joining the hands of political leaders Manley and Seaga (right) during a performance at the National Stadium in 1978.

Seaga: Bob was no ordinary man

PRIME MINISTER EDWARD SEAGA in a tribute to the late reggae star Bob Marley, described him as a giant among musicians and men.

He said that the death of the entertainer was not only Jamaica's loss, but the world's and said that solace could be taken in the fact that he left a rich heritage of popular Jamaican music.

The statement said:

"Bob Marley, Jamaica's international reggae superstar, friend of the poor and the weak, who inspired the Jamaican youth to new heights in popular music, passed away in Miami today at the youthful age of 36.

"Bob was on his way home to Jamaica from West Germany where he had been for medical treatment.

"Bob Marley was no ordinary musician or ordinary man.

"His music did more than entertain. He translated into music, in a remarkable, inimitable style, the aspirations, pain and feeling of millions of people throughout the world. He gave them great hopes for peace and love.

"He was the unapologetic spokesman for a generation who languished for a better world and his admirers ranged from the poverty-stricken in Kingston, New York, London, Paris and other parts of the world to the affluent.

"As an individual, Bob Marley was the embodiment of discipline and he personified hard work and determination to reach his goals. Without these attributes which he demonstrated so much he could not have reached the stars in the world of popular music.

"His talent would have been wasted if he had not worked hard and developed it to perfection. His life was an outstanding example to ghetto youth.

"His influence on children was profound. And he always showed his concern and love for them.

"Bob was indeed a giant among musicians and men.

"He began his journey to stardom in the sixties, when the Wailers was formed. At that time the nation realised that it was fortunate in having 'traditional' singers in modern garb. These were difficult years, but with perseverance in pursuing his artistic goals he gained the heart of the nation.

"When Jamaica became independent, he was among those who provided a beacon of hope striving to overcome obstacles. How well do we remember songs like 'Simmer Down' and 'One Love' that provided a message while they entertained.

"In 1975 Bob Marley entered the international music scene with the album 'Catch A Fire'. This was a big step in the series of developments that have seen Marley, a self-taught artist, emerge as a singer, composer and musician of world renown.

"The albums that followed were of a consistently high calibre: 'Rastaman Vibration' and 'Exodus' to name only two.

"It was just recently that he was awarded the Order of Merit, the nation's third highest honour, for his international contributions to music.

"Bob's death is not only Jamaica's loss but the world's loss. But we can take solace in the fact that he left with us a rich heritage of popular Jamaican music. He has passed on but his music and spirit live on.

"On behalf of the Government and people of Jamaica I extend deep sympathy and condolence to his family, and particularly to his widow Mrs. Rita Marley and the children.

"I should like to end this tribute by pointing out that Bob recently wrote a song called "I Know" which is soon to be released on record. Rita has asked me to share with you a verse from this song.

"When the race is hard to run
And you just can't stand the pace
All I know is that Jah will be
Waiting there. I know".

MARLEY AN OUTSTANDING MESSENGER, SAYS BARTLETT

The Minister of State in the Prime Minister's Office with responsibility for Information and Culture, the Hon. Edmund Bartlett, in a statement Tuesday, on the death of reggae singer Bob Marley, described him as "an out standing messenger of peace".

Mr. Bartlett's statement read:

"It is with deep sadness that we learnt of the death of Jamaica's world famous Reggae Super Star, the Honourable Bob Marley in Miami.

"The news is even more painful when we realize how close he was to us on his journey home.

"We, in Jamaica, have read with pride of Bob Marley's unmatched achievements on stages all over the world. His concerts that drew record crowds even in lands where his was a foreign language.

"We rejoiced when his songs about the beliefs, aspirations and feelings of thousands of ghetto youth whose way of life he knew so well, touched the hearts of millions around the world.

"Bob never forgot his people. He always remembered those among whom he lived and grew, as a man and as a musician. He gave of his talent, his time and his worldly goods to help spread the message of peace, love and hope, as well as to assist in the development of talent among those who might otherwise have remained hidden and unknown.

As a Rastafarian, Bob was the embodiment of their beliefs and their constant faith in the all embracing love, benevolence and power of the Creator.

"The Honourable Mr. Marley is no longer with us in the flesh, but Jamaica continues to be richer because he lived. His contributions will still inspire and enrich the people of the land he loved so well.

"We express sincere condolences to all the family and loved ones of the Honourable Robert Marley. We mourn with you the loss of a dear one, but we remember too that for him, 'death is a door that leads to light'."

THURSDAY, MAY 21, 1981

A Jamaican legend, Marley is buried (with his Bible and Gibson guitar placed in the coffin) with full state honors in St. Ann Parish after thousands, including Prime Minister Edward Seaga, attend an Ethiopian Orthodox festival funeral at the National Heroes Arena in Kingston. His body is driven the 43 miles back to Nine Miles, his childhood home, where it is interred in a mausoleum.

Die jamaikanische Legende Bob Marley wird (zusammen mit seiner Bibel und seiner Gibson-Gitarre) mit staatlichen Ehren in St. Ann Parish beigesetzt, nachdem Tausende, darunter auch der Premierminister Edward Seaga, an einer äthiopisch-orthodoxen Trauerfeier in der National Heroes Arena in Kingston teilgenommen haben. Sein Leichnam wird ins 70 Kilometer entfernte Nine Miles gebracht, wo er aufwuchs, und in einem Mausoleum beigesetzt.

Légende jamaïcaine, Bob Marley est enterré à Saint Ann avec tous les honneurs officiels ; des milliers de personnes, parmi lesquelles le Premier ministre Edward Seaga, ont assisté auparavant au service funéraire orthodoxe éthiopien qui s'est tenu à la National Heroes Arena de Kingston. Son corps a ensuite été conduit sur une soixantaine de kilomètres jusqu'à Nine Miles, la maison de son enfance, où il est inhumé dans un mausolée. Sa bible et sa guitare Gibson sont placées dans son cercueil.

"Bob Marley was never seen. He was an experience which left an indelible imprint with each encounter. Such a man cannot be erased from the mind. He is part of the collective consciousness of the nation."

„Bob Marley konnte man nicht nur mit den Augen wahrnehmen. Er war eine Erfahrung, die bei jeder Begegnung einen nachhaltigen Eindruck hinterließ. Solch ein Mensch kann nicht aus der Erinnerung verschwinden. Er ist Teil des kollektiven Bewusstseins unserer Nation."

« Bob Marley, personne ne peut prétendre le résumer. Le rencontrer était à chaque fois une expérience qui laissait une empreinte indélébile. Un tel homme ne peut être effacé des esprits. Il fait partie de la conscience collective de la nation. »

PRIME MINISTER EDWARD SEAGA

"His message was a protest against injustice, a comfort for the oppressed. He stood there, performed there, his message reached there and everywhere. Today's funeral service is an international rite of a native son. He was born in a humble cottage nine miles from Alexandria in the parish of St. Ann. He lived in the western section of Kingston as a boy, where he joined in the struggle of the ghetto. He learned the message of survival in his boyhood days in Kingston's west end. But it was his raw talent, unswerving discipline, and sheer perseverance that transported him from just another victim of the ghetto to the top-ranking superstar in the entertainment industry of the third world."

„Seine Botschaft war ein Protest gegen Ungerechtigkeit, ein Trost für die Unterdrückten. Dort stand er, dort sang er, dort und überall wurde seine Botschaft gehört. Die Trauerfeier am heutigen Tage ist ein internationaler Ritus für einen Sohn unseres Landes. Geboren wurde er in einer bescheidenen Hütte neun Meilen von Alexandria entfernt in der Gemeinde St. Ann. Als Junge lernte er im westlichen Teil Kingstons das harte Leben des Ghettos kennen. In seiner Jugend erfuhr er im Westend von Kingston,

was Überleben bedeutete. Dank seines unglaublichen Talents, seiner eisernen Disziplin und seiner Beharrlichkeit verwandelte er sich von einem Opfer des Ghettos in den größten Superstar in der Unterhaltungsbranche der Dritten Welt."

« Son message était une protestation contre l'injustice, un réconfort pour les opprimés. Il s'est tenu ici, il a chanté ici, son message a touché les gens, ici et partout. Le service funéraire d'aujourd'hui est un rite international dédié à un enfant du pays. Il est né dans une modeste masure à neuf miles d'Alexandria, dans la paroisse de Saint Ann. Enfant, il a grandi dans la partie ouest de Kingston, où il s'est joint aux habitants du ghetto en lutte. C'est dans les quartiers ouest de Kingston, pendant ses années d'enfance, qu'il a appris la valeur de la survie. Mais c'est grâce à son talent brut, à sa discipline indéfectible et à sa persévérance qu'il n'est pas devenu une énième victime du ghetto mais la plus grande personnalité de l'industrie du divertissement dans le tiers-monde. »
JAMAICAN GOVERNOR GENERAL MICHAEL MANLEY

WEDNESDAY, DECEMBER 29, 1982
The Jamaican Postal Service issues a set of five commemorative stamps and a souvenir sheet in honor of Bob Marley.

Die jamaikanische Post gibt eine Serie mit fünf Briefmarken und einen Block zu Ehren von Bob Marley heraus.

Les services postaux jamaïcains éditent une série de cinq timbres et un carnet souvenir en hommage à Bob Marley.

MONDAY, MAY 28, 1984

Bob Marley and The Wailers' retrospective collection, the 14-track **Legend**, is certified as double platinum by the British Phonographic Industry. Marley is more popular (in terms of record sales) dead than alive, and his legacy will continue to grow, with **Legend** becoming one of the most enduring catalog items of the next 25 years. Although he only scored one United States **Billboard** Hot 100 chart placement while fronting The Wailers (*Roots, Rock, Reggae*, which peaked at number 56), the incomplete album **Anthology** will spend more than two years on the United States album chart, eventually racking up more than 10 million sales stateside.

Das posthum erschienene Album **Legend** von Bob Marley and The Wailers mit 14 Titeln erhält von der British Phonographic Industry zweifaches Platin. Gemessen an den Verkaufszahlen ist Marley tot populärer als lebendig. Sein Ruhm wird immer größer und **Legend** entwickelt sich im Laufe der nächsten 25 Jahre zu einem der beständigsten Titel der Backlist.

Als Frontmann der Wailers schaffte es Marley nur einmal in die US **Billboard** Hot 100 (*Roots, Rock, Reggae* auf Platz 56 der Charts); das unvollständig gebliebene Album **Anthology** verharrte über zwei Jahre lang in den US-Charts und verkaufte sich in den Staaten insgesamt über 10 Millionen Mal.

L'Industrie phonographique britannique annonce que la collection rétrospective de Bob Marley and The Wailers, un album de 14 titres intitulé **Legend**, est double disque de platine. Marley est plus populaire mort que de son vivant (en termes de vente de disques) et son héritage continuera de croître : au cours des 25 années suivantes, **Legend** deviendra un classique. Alors qu'il n'avait fait entrer qu'un seul titre dans le Top 100 américain (**Billboard** Hot 100) avec les Wailers (*Roots, Rock, Reggae*, qui n'avait jamais dépassé la 56e place), l'album inachevé **Anthology** restera plus de deux ans dans le classement américain et se vendra à plus de dix millions d'exemplaires dans le pays.

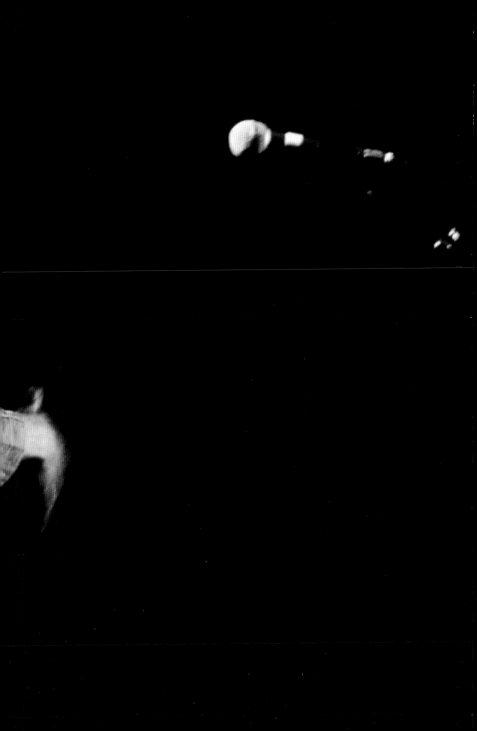

SUNDAY, MAY 11, 1986
The former location of both his residence and the
Tuff Gong studio, the Bob Marley Museum, located at
56 Hope Road, Kingston 6, opens to the public.

Das Bob Marley Museum öffnet seine Pforten in
dem Gebäude an der 56 Hope Road, Kingston 6, das
ehemals sein Wohnhaus und Sitz des Tuff Gong Studios war.

Le bâtiment qui abritait à la fois le logement des
Marley et les studios Tuff Gong, au 56 Hope Road,
Kingston 6, transformé en Musée Bob Marley, ouvre
ses portes au public.

JULY 1988

Ziggy Marley and The Melody Makers—comprising Ziggy, Cedella, Sharon, and Stephen—hit the United States charts with the Tina Weymouth/Chris Frantz–produced **Conscious Party**; *Tomorrow People*, a song from the album, is a Top 40 hit in both the United States and the United Kingdom.

Ziggy Marley and The Melody Makers - bestehend aus Ziggy, Cedella, Sharon und Stephen - stürmen die amerikanischen Charts mit dem von Tina Weymouth und Chris Frantz produzierten Album **Conscious Party**; eines der Stücke, *Tomorrow People*, ist in England und in den Staaten ein Top-Forty-Hit.

Ziggy Marley et les Melody Makers - Ziggy, Cedella, Sharon et Stephen - entrent dans le classement américain des meilleures ventes de singles avec l'album **Conscious Party**, produit par Tina Weymouth et Chris Frantz. *Tomorrow People*, une autre chanson de l'album, intègre le Top 40 américain et britannique.

THE 1990ˢ

DIE 1990ER

LES ANNÉES 1990

TUESDAY, FEBRUARY 6, 1990
A national holiday is proclaimed in Jamaica to com-
memorate the 45th anniversary of Bob Marley's birth.
Anlässlich von Bob Marleys 45. Geburtstag wird der
6. Februar in Jamaika zum offiziellen Feiertag erklärt.
À l'occasion du 45ᵉ anniversaire de sa naissance, un
jour férié est institué en Jamaïque à la mémoire de
Bob Marley.

JUNE 1990
Chris Blackwell inaugurates The Bob Marley
Memorial Fund in New York by presenting a check for
$75,000 to Amnesty International. (The donation will
be given annually for 10 years at the Penta Hotel in
New York.) Island reissues CD versions of 13 Marley
albums in the United States.
Chris Blackwell eröffnet den Bob Marley Memorial
Fund in New York mit der Überreichung eines 75.000-
Dollar-Schecks an Amnesty International. Die Spende
wird in den nächsten zehn Jahren alljährlich im Penta
Hotel in New York überreicht. Island bringt in Amerika
13 Marley-Alben auf CD heraus.
Chris Blackwell inaugure le Bob Marley Memorial
Fund à New York en versant un chèque de 75 000
dollars à Amnesty International. (Ce don sera réitéré
chaque année pendant dix ans au cours d'une soirée
donnée au Penta Hotel de New York.) Island réédite
les treize albums de Marley en CD pour les États-Unis.

TUESDAY, JULY 2, 1991

Reggae veteran Eddy Grant joins the heated competition to wrest control of Bob Marley's recording and publishing legacy by bidding $13.5 million for the rights, which have also attracted a $15.2 million bid by MCA Records and a joint offer by Rita Marley and Blackwell. Rita issues the following statement: "We are completely incensed as a family at the idea of Eddy Grant trying to take our heritage away." The Jamaican Supreme Court continues to consider the various tenders. The court session will be adjourned until October, with the ruling that the three offers were too disparate for comparison.

Der Reggae-Veteran Eddy Grant ist eine der Parteien, die sich in den hitzigen Kampf um Bob Marleys Hinterlassenschaft an Schallplattenaufnahmen und Veröffentlichungen stürzen: Er bietet 13,5 Mio. Dollar für die Rechte, MCA Records haben 15,2 Mio. geboten, ein gemeinsames Angebot von Rita Marley und Blackwell liegt ebenfalls vor. Rita gibt die folgende Erklärung ab: „Wir als Familie sind entrüstet über die Vorstellung, dass Eddy Grant versucht, unser Erbe zu stehlen." Der oberste Gerichtshof Jamaikas berät über die verschiedenen Angebote. Das Gericht vertagt sich bis Oktober mit der Begründung, dass die drei Angebote zu verschieden seien, um sie vergleichen zu können.

Le vétéran du reggae Eddy Grant se lance dans la compétition acharnée pour le contrôle des enregistrements et publications de Bob Marley. Il fait une offre à 13,5 millions de dollars pour en acquérir les droits ; MCA Records propose 15,2 millions de dollars, tandis que Rita Marley et Blackwell font une offre conjointe bien inférieure. Rita rédige un communiqué : « Nous sommes totalement scandalisés, en tant que famille, à l'idée qu'Eddy Grant tente de nous déshériter. » La Cour suprême de la Jamaïque examine longuement ces trois propositions ; elle reporte sa décision à octobre mais celle-ci reste sans effet, les trois offres étant jugées trop divergentes pour être comparées.

MONDAY, DECEMBER 9, 1991

Jamaican Supreme Court Justice Clarence Walker, ending a decade of legal wrangles, directs that Bob Marley's assets be sold for $11.5 million to his widow, children, and Chris Blackwell's Island Logic Ltd., despite MCA's higher offer. Ziggy Marley names his daughter, born today, Justice.

Der Richter des obersten Gerichtshofs Jamaikas, Clarence Walker, beendet ein Jahrzehnt der Rechtsstreitigkeiten und verfügt, dass die Rechte an Bob Marleys Hinterlassenschaft für 11,5 Mio. Dollar an seine Witwe, seine Kinder und Chris Blackwells Island Logic Ltd. gehen, trotz des höheren Gebotes von MCA. Ziggy Marley nennt seine an diesem Tag geborene Tochter Justice (Gerechtigkeit).

Le juge Clarence Walker de la Cour suprême jamaïcaine met fin à dix ans de querelle juridique : les biens de Marley seront finalement vendus pour 11,5 millions de dollars à sa veuve, à ses enfants et à la compagnie de Chris Blackwell, Island Logic Ltd. La fille de Ziggy Marley, née ce jour-là, est baptisée Justice.

SATURDAY, OCTOBER 3, 1992

Song Of Freedom, a four-CD retrospective collection featuring Marley's first recordings in 1962, a live version of *Redemption Song* recorded at his final concert in Pittsburgh, Pennsylvania, in September 1980, his numerous hits, and previously unavailable cuts unearthed by Rita, is simultaneously released in 54 countries. The 78-track release is accompanied by a 64-page tribute booklet written by **Billboard** editor Timothy White (who is also the author of **Catch A Fire**, a Marley tome).

Auf *Song Of Freedom*, einem Set von vier CDs, findet sich Marleys erste Plattenaufnahme aus dem Jahr 1962, eine Live-Version von *Redemption Song*, die bei seinem letzten Auftritt in Pittsburgh, Pennsylvania, im September 1980 aufgenommen wurde, seine vielen Hits sowie bisher unveröffentlichte Tracks, die Rita

ausgegraben hat. Die Box wird gleichzeitig in 54 Ländern auf den Markt gebracht, die 78 Titel werden von einem 64-seitigen Booklet begleitet, einer Hommage an Bob Marley von **Billboard**-Herausgeber Timothy White, Autor der Marley-Biografie **Catch A Fire**.

Song Of Freedom, un coffret de quatre CD contenant les premiers enregistrements de Marley datant de 1962, une version live de *Redemption Song* enregistrée lors de son dernier concert à Pittsburgh (Pennsylvanie) en septembre 1980, ses chansons les plus connues et des versions inédites exhumées par Rita, sort simultanément dans 54 pays. Les 78 titres sont accompagnés d'un livret de 64 pages rédigé par le rédacteur en chef de **Billboard**, Timothy White (également auteur d'une biographie de Marley intitulée **Catch A Fire**).

"*I know claiming Bob Marley as Irish might be a little difficult, but bear with me. Jamaica and Ireland have lots in common. Chris Blackwell, weeds, lots of green weeds. Religion. The philosophy of procrastination ('don't put off till tomorrow what you can put off till the day after'), unless of course it's freedom ... He wanted everything at the same time and was everything at the same time: prophet, soul rebel, Rastaman, herbsman, wild man, a natural mystic man, ladies' man, island man, family man, Rita's man, soccer man, showman, shaman, human, Jamaican!*"

„*Ich weiß, dass es wahrscheinlich auf einen gewissen Unglauben stoßen wird, wenn ich behaupte, dass Bob Marley Ire war, aber warten Sie's ab. Jamaika und Irland haben viel gemeinsam. Chris Blackwell, Gras, sehr viel grünes Gras. Religion. Der Glaube an die Faulheit (‚verschiebe nichts auf morgen, was du nicht auch auf übermorgen verschieben kannst'), außer natürlich, wenn es um die Freiheit geht ... Er wollte alles gleichzeitig und war alles gleichzeitig: Prophet, Soul-Rebell, Rastaman, Kiffer, wilder Mann, Naturmystiker, Mann der Frauen, Inselmann, Familienmann, Ritas Mann, Fußballmann, Showman, Schamane, Mensch, Jamaikaner!*"

« *Je sais qu'il est assez difficile d'affirmer que Bob Marley est Irlandais, mais je sollicite votre indulgence. La Jamaïque et l'Irlande ont beaucoup de choses en commun : Chris Blackwell, la mauvaise herbe (des champs entiers de mauvaise herbe !), la religion, la procrastination ("Ne remets pas à demain ce que tu peux faire après-demain") et surtout, bien sûr, la soif de liberté... Il voulait tout à la fois et il était tout à la fois : prophète, âme rebelle, rastaman, homme de l'herbe, homme sauvage, homme mystique par nature, homme à femmes, homme d'une île, homme de famille, l'homme de Rita, footballeur, showman, chaman, humain, Jamaïcain !* »

BONO

WEDNESDAY, JANUARY 19, 1994

Bob Marley is posthumously inducted into the Rock and Roll Hall of Fame at the ninth annual dinner held at New York's Waldorf-Astoria Hotel. His widow, Rita, accepts the award from inductor Bono.

Bob Marley wird beim neunten Jahresdinner im New Yorker Waldorf-Astoria Hotel posthum in die Rock and Roll Hall of Fame aufgenommen. Seine Witwe Rita nimmt die Ehrung von Laudator Bono entgegen.

Bob Marley fait son entrée à titre posthume au Rock and Roll Hall of Fame lors du neuvième dîner annuel qui se tient à l'hôtel Waldorf-Astoria de New York. Sa veuve, Rita, reçoit le prix des mains de Bono.

SUNDAY, FEBRUARY 6, 1994

A year of festivities to celebrate the 50th anniversary of Marley's birth begins at the Bob Marley Museum in Kingston with the Marley Foundation's tribute concert.

Ein Jahr der Feste zur Feier von Marleys 50. Geburtstag beginnt im Bob Marley Museum in Kingston mit einem Konzert zugunsten der Marley Foundation.

Lancement d'une année de célébrations organisées pour le 50ᵉ anniversaire de Marley au Musée Bob Marley, à Kingston, avec un concert au profit de la Fondation Marley.

WEDNESDAY, FEBRUARY 26, 1997

The Fugees perform a tribute to Bob Marley with members of the Marley clan at the 39th annual Grammy Awards, held at New York's Madison Square Garden.

The Fugees spielen zusammen mit Mitgliedern des Marley-Clans bei der 39. Verleihung der Grammy Awards im New Yorker Madison Square Garden eine Hommage an Bob Marley.

Les Fugees jouent en hommage à Bob Marley avec plusieurs membres du clan Marley lors de la 39e cérémonie des Grammy Awards, au Madison Square Garden de New York.

THURSDAY, DECEMBER 10, 1998

Further evidence of Marley's enduring legacy is noted with an all-star rendition of his *Get Up, Stand Up* at Amnesty International's "The Struggle Continues" concert at Bercy Stadium in Paris, France. The concert, celebrating the 50th anniversary of the Universal Declaration of Human Rights, features Bruce Springsteen, Alanis Morissette, Peter Gabriel, Radiohead, Shania Twain, Tracy Chapman, Jimmy Page and Robert Plant, Asian Dub Foundation, French Antilles–based world music aggregate Kassav, and Youssou N'Dour.

Marleys nachhaltiger Einfluss ist beim Amnesty International-Konzert „The Struggle Continues" zu spüren, als ein All-Star-Aufgebot sein *Get Up, Stand Up* im Bercy Stadion in Paris singt. Bei dem Konzert, mit dem 50 Jahre Allgemeine Erklärung der Menschenrechte gefeiert werden, treten Bruce Springsteen,

Alanis Morissette, Peter Gabriel, Radiohead, Shania Twain, Tracy Chapman, Jimmy Page und Robert Plant, die Asian Dub Foundation, Kassav', das Worldmusic-Kollektiv von den französischen Antillen, und Youssou N'Dour auf.

Le message de Marley est toujours porté à travers le monde : à Paris, sur la scène de Bercy, une ribambelle de stars de la chanson reprennent *Get Up, Stand Up* lors du concert baptisé « La lutte continue » organisé par Amnesty International pour célébrer le 50e anniversaire de la Déclaration universelle des droits de l'homme. Parmi les artistes à l'affiche figurent Bruce Springsteen, Alanis Morissette, Peter Gabriel, Radiohead, Shania Twain, Tracy Chapman, Jimmy Page et Robert Plant, Asian Dub Foundation, Kassav et Youssou N'Dour.

SATURDAY, FEBRUARY 6, 1999

"Bob Marley: A Tribute To Freedom" opens at Universal CityWalk in Orlando, Florida. The permanent exhibition includes a re-creation of Marley's Hope Road house in Kingston, with paintings, photos, and videos; a gazebo for reggae acts to perform; and a restaurant.

Die Dauerausstellung „Bob Marley: A Tribute to Freedom" wird im Universal CityWalk in Orlando, Florida, eröffnet. Zu sehen sind eine Nachbildung von Marleys Haus an der Hope Road in Kingston, Gemälde, Fotos und Videos, es gibt einen Pavillon, in dem Reggae-Bands auftreten können, und ein Restaurant.

L'Universal CityWalk d'Orlando (Floride) inaugure «Bob Marley: A Tribute to Freedom», une exposition permanente qui présente une reproduction de la maison de Marley sur Hope Road, à Kingston, ainsi que des peintures, des photos et des vidéos, une estrade pouvant accueillir des concerts de reggae et un restaurant.

SATURDAY, DECEMBER 4, 1999

Organized by one of his sons, Stephen Marley, "One Love: The Bob Marley All-Star Tribute" takes place on James Bond Beach in Oracabessa, St. Mary, in Jamaica. The show features Erykah Badu, Tracy Chapman, Jimmy Cliff, Ben Harper, Lauryn Hill, Chrissie Hynde, Queen Latifah, Rita and Stephen Marley, Ziggy Marley and The Melody Makers, The Wailers, Dr. John, emerging female rapper Eve, Busta Rhymes, The Black Crowes' Chris Robinson, and Darius Rucker.

Das von Marleys Sohn Stephen organisierte Festival „One Love: The Bob Marley All-Star Tribute" findet am James Bond Beach in Oracabessa, St. Mary, auf Jamaika statt. Es spielen Erykah Badu, Tracy Chapman, Jimmy Cliff, Ben Harper, Lauryn Hill, Chrissie Hynde, Queen Latifah, Rita und Stephen Marley, Ziggy Marley and The Melody Makers, The Wailers, Dr. John, die junge Rapperin Eve, Busta Rhymes, Chris Robinson von den Black Crowes und Darius Rucker.

Stephen Marley, un de ses fils, organise le concert «One Love: The Bob Marley All-Star Tribute» sur la James Bond Beach d'Oracabessa, à Saint Mary (Jamaïque), auquel participent Erykah Badu, Tracy Chapman, Jimmy Cliff, Ben Harper, Lauryn Hill, Chrissie Hynde, Queen Latifah, Rita et Stephen Marley, Ziggy Marley et les Melody Makers, les Wailers, Dr. John, la jeune rappeuse Eve, Busta Rhymes, Chris Robinson des Black Crowes et Darius Rucker.

FRIDAY, DECEMBER 31, 1999
Time magazine heralds **Exodus** as Best Album of the Century: " ... every song is a classic, from the messages of love to the anthems of revolution. But more than that, the album is a political and cultural nexus, drawing inspiration from the third world and then giving voice to it the world over." The runners-up? Miles Davis' **Kind Of Blue** and Jimi Hendrix's **Are You Experienced?**

Das amerikanische **Time**-Magazin bezeichnet **Exodus** als das beste Album des Jahrhunderts: „ ... jeder Song ist ein Klassiker, von den Botschaften der Liebe bis hin zu den Revolutionshymnen. Doch darüber hinaus ist das Album ein politischer und kultureller Knotenpunkt, der aus der Dritten Welt Inspiration bezieht und ihr weltweit eine Stimme verleiht." Auf den nächsten Plätzen landen Miles Davis' **Kind Of Blue** und Jimi Hendrixs **Are You Experienced?**

Le magazine **Time** sacre **Exodus** «Meilleur album du siècle»: «Chaque chanson est un classique, depuis les messages d'amour jusqu'aux hymnes révolutionnaires. Mais surtout, l'album est un forum politique et culturel, qui s'inspire du tiers-monde et fait entendre sa voix de par le monde.» Les albums classés deuxième et troisième sont **Kind Of Blue** de Miles Davis et **Are You Experienced?** de Jimi Hendrix.

THE 2000ˢ

SEIT 2000

LES ANNÉES 2000

SUNDAY, JANUARY 1, 2004

The Bob Marley Foundation is announced with its new website at www.bobmarleyfoundation.org. Established by Rita Marley and the Marley family, its stated mission is "to maintain a dynamic foundation which will enable individuals, groups, and/or communities in developing nations, particularly Jamaica and Africa, to create and implement programs that assist in the empowerment of the oppressed and the elimination of generational poverty through sustainable projects." An entirely redesigned official Bob Marley website will be launched on November 30, 2006, at www.bobmarley.com.

Die Bob Marley Foundation stellt sich mit ihrer neuen Website www.bobmarleyfoundation.org vor. Die von Rita Marley und der Familie Marley gegründete Stiftung verfolgt das Ziel, „eine dynamische Stiftung zu unterhalten, die Einzelpersonen, Gruppen und/oder Gemeinschaften in Entwicklungsländern, insbesondere in Jamaika und Afrika, in die Lage versetzt, Programme zu entwickeln und durchzuführen, die zur Ermächtigung der Unterdrückten und Eliminierung der generationenübergreifenden Armut durch nachhaltige Projekte beiträgt." Eine komplett neu gestaltete offizielle Bob-Marley-Website wird am 30. November 2006 unter www.bobmarley.com ins Netz gestellt.

La Fondation Bob Marley crée son site Internet, www.bobmarleyfoundation.org. Créée par Rita Marley et la famille Marley, sa mission est de «faire vivre une fondation dynamique qui permette aux individus, aux groupes et aux communautés des pays en voie de développement, en particulier en Jamaïque et en Afrique, de développer des programmes qui contribuent à donner davantage de pouvoir aux opprimés et à éradiquer la pauvreté endémique au travers de projets durables». Un tout nouveau site officiel de Bob Marley sera lancé le 30 novembre 2006: www.bobmarley.com.

WEDNESDAY, JANUARY 19, 2005

Following his posthumous Grammy Lifetime Achievement Award in 2001, Marley's enduring No Woman, No Cry becomes one of the latest additions into the Grammy Hall of Fame.

Nachdem Marley 2001 bereits posthum der Grammy Lifetime Achievement Award verliehen wurde, geht sein Klassiker No Woman, No Cry nun auch in die Grammy Hall of Fame ein.

L'académie des Grammies, qui lui a décerné un prix d'honneur pour l'ensemble de sa carrière en 2001, fait entrer No Woman, No Cry dans son célèbre Hall of Fame.

SUNDAY, FEBRUARY 6, 2005
The "Celebrating African Unity" concert, marking what would have been Marley's 60th birthday, takes place in Meskel Square in Addis Ababa, Ethiopia. Rita Marley and Bob Marley's five sons are joined by Lauryn Hill, Angelique Kidjo, Baaba Maal, and Youssou N'Dour in the concert, organized by The Bob Marley Foundation.

Das Konzert „Celebrating African Unity" an Marleys 60. Geburtstag findet auf dem Meskel Square in Addis Abeba, Äthiopien, statt. Rita Marley und die fünf Marley-Söhne spielen neben Lauryn Hill, Angelique Kidjo, Baaba Maal und Youssou N'Dour bei dem Konzert, das von der Bob Marley Foundation organisiert wurde.

Le concert « Celebrating African Unity » organisé par la Fondation Bob Marley, qui marque le 60ᵉ anniversaire de la naissance de Bob Marley, se tient sur la place Meskel d'Addis Ababa, en Éthiopie. Les cinq fils de Rita et Bob Marley sont accompagnés de Lauryn Hill, Angelique Kidjo, Baaba Maal et Youssou N'Dour.

"Let's be blunt. He's still the world's biggest rock star."
„Wir können es ohne Umschweife sagen: Er ist nach wie vor der größte Rockstar der Welt."
« Soyons francs. Il reste à ce jour la plus grande rock star du monde. »
ENTERTAINMENT WEEKLY

AUGUST 2006
The Bank of Jamaica issues a limited edition of 1,000 gold and silver coins celebrating Marley's 60th birthday—some 18 months after the event. The commemorative coins, made by the British Royal Mint, sell for $100 (£55) each.

Die Bank of Jamaika gibt anlässlich von Marleys 60. Geburtstag eine limitierte Edition von 1000 Gold- und Silbermünzen heraus – mit ungefähr 18-monatiger Ver-

spätung. Die von der British Royal Mint geprägten Gedenkmünzen werden für 55 Pfund das Stück verkauft.

La Bank of Jamaica édite une série limitée de 1 000 pièces d'or et d'argent célébrant le 60ᵉ anniversaire de Marley – quelque 18 mois après la date. Ces pièces commémoratives, fondues par les Forges Royales britanniques, sont vendues 55 livres.

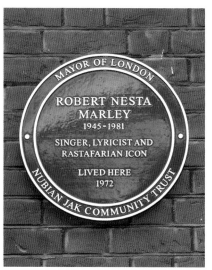

THURSDAY, OCTOBER 26, 2006
A heritage plaque is unveiled at 34 Ridgmount Gardens in Bloomsbury, London—the first place Marley lived when he came to England in 1972.

Am Haus 34 Ridgmount Gardens in Bloomsbury, London, wird eine Gedenktafel enthüllt – hier war Marleys erster Wohnort, als er 1972 nach England kam.

Une plaque est dévoilée au 34 Ridgmount Gardens, à Bloomsbury (Londres) - le premier endroit où a vécu Marley lorsqu'il a séjourné en Angleterre en 1972.

"Like many people I have appreciated and admired the work of Bob Marley for decades. He was quite simply a musical genius, and he remains a much loved international, iconic reggae artist. I am proud that we will now have a plaque in his honor in London, officially marking the remarkable achievements of this hugely talented man."

„Wie viele andere Menschen auch schätze und bewundere ich das Werk von Bob Marley seit Jahrzehnten. Er war ein musikalisches Genie und ist und bleibt ein legendärer und von vielen verehrter Reggaekünstler. Ich bin stolz darauf, dass wir jetzt ihm zu Ehren eine Gedenktafel in London haben, mit der die herausragenden Leistungen dieses ungemein begabten Mannes offiziell gewürdigt werden."

« Comme beaucoup de gens, j'apprécie et j'admire l'œuvre de Bob Marley depuis des dizaines d'années. Il était tout simplement un génie musical, et il demeure un artiste de reggae légendaire et très aimé dans le monde entier. Je suis fier que nous ayons désormais une plaque en son honneur à Londres, afin de saluer officiellement la réussite de cet homme immensément talentueux. »
KEN LIVINGSTONE, MAYOR OF LONDON

FRIDAY, MARCH 7, 2008

Marley's official website confirms that movie producers Harvey and Bob Weinstein are to produce a Marley biopic based on Rita Marley's book, **No Woman No Cry: My Life With Bob Marley**, for release in 2010, while film director Martin Scorsese continues preparations for a documentary film about the reggae icon. Citing scheduling conflicts, Scorsese will be replaced by director Jonathan Demme later in the year.

Auf Marleys offizieller Website wird bestätigt, dass die Produzenten Harvey und Bob Weinstein einen Film über Marley drehen lassen wollen, der auf Rita Marleys **No Woman No Cry: Mein Leben mit Bob Marley** basiert. Als Filmstart wird 2010 anvisiert. Regisseur Martin Scorsese ist mit den Vorarbeiten für einen neuen Dokumentarfilm über die Reggae-Ikone beschäftigt. Wegen Terminschwierigkeiten wird Scorsese im Laufe des Jahres durch Regisseur Jonathan Demme ersetzt.

Le site officiel de Marley confirme que les rois du cinéma hollywoodien Harvey et Bob Weinstein vont produire un film sur la vie de Marley d'après le livre de Rita Marley, **No Woman No Cry : ma vie avec Bob Marley**. La sortie du film est prévue pour 2010, alors que le réalisateur Martin Scorsese continue à préparer un film documentaire sur l'icône du reggae. Scorsese, qui évoque des problèmes d'emploi du temps, sera remplacé par le réalisateur Jonathan Demme quelque temps plus tard.

3

ESSENTIAL RECORDINGS

DIE WICHTIGSTEN ALBEN

PRINCIPAUX ENREGISTREMENTS

SIMMER DOWN AT STUDIO ONE, VOL. 1 (1994)

1 This Train **2** Simmer Down **3** I Am Going Home **4** Do You Remember **5** Mr. Talkative **6** Habits **7** Amen **8** Go Jimmy Go **9** Teenager In Love **10** I Need You **11** It Hurts To Be Alone **12** True Confession **13** Lonesome Feeling **14** There She Goes **15** Diamond Baby **16** Playboy **17** Where's The Girl For Me **18** Hooligan **19** One Love **20** Love And Affection

SOUL REBELS (1971)

1 Soul Rebel **2** Try Me **3** It's Alright **4** No Sympathy **5** My Cup **6** Soul Almighty **7** Rebel's Hop **8** Corner Stone **9** 400 Years **10** No Water **11** Reaction **12** My Sympathy **13** Dreamland **14** Dreamland (Version) **15** Dracula **16** Soul Rebel (Version 4) **17** Version Of Cup **18** Zig Zag **19** Jah Is Mighty **20** Brand New Second Hand **21** Brand New Second Hand (Version) **22** Downpresser

CATCH A FIRE (1972)

1 Concrete Jungle **2** Slave Driver **3** 400 Years **4** Stop That Train **5** Baby We've Got A Date (Rock It Baby) **6** Stir It Up **7** Kinky Reggae **8** No More Trouble **9** Midnight Ravers **10** High Tide Or Low Tide **11** All Day All Night

AFRICAN HERBSMAN (1973)

1 Lively Up Yourself **2** Small Axe **3** Duppy Conqueror **4** Trench Town Rock **5** African Herbsman **6** Keep On Moving **7** Fussing And Fighting **8** Stand Alone **9** All In One **10** Don't Rock The Boat **11** Put It On **12** Sun Is Shining **13** Kaya **14** Riding High **15** Brain Washing **16** 400 Years

"Burnin' is a heavily committed album, both politically and religiously, reflecting what a lot of us had maybe overlooked—that Marley is an angry young man with a mission."
MELODY MAKER ON BURNIN'

"Natty Dread wrangled the seemingly unreconcilable impulses of reggae—its economy of line and expansiveness of spirit—into an intense evocation of a people's boundless capacities for faith, anger and love."
ROLLING STONE
ON NATTY DREAD

BURNIN' (1973)
1 Get Up, Stand Up **2** Hallelujah Time **3** I Shot The Sheriff **4** Burnin' And Lootin' **5** Put It On **6** Small Axe **7** Pass It On **8** Duppy Conqueror **9** One Foundation **10** Rastaman Chant

NATTY DREAD (1974)
1 Lively Up Yourself **2** No Woman, No Cry **3** Them Belly Full (But We Hungry) **4** Rebel Music (Three O'Clock Roadblock) **5** So Jah S'eh **6** Natty Dread **7** Bend Down Low **8** Talkin' Blues **9** Revolution **10** Am-A-Do

"The greatest live album of all time? The atmosphere of jubilation is palpable."
MOJO ON LIVE!

"Live! is an enticing glimpse into the Wailers rousing stage act, showcasing Marleys vocal spontaneity and the rhythm sections funky, organic drive."
DOWNBEAT ON LIVE!

RASTA REVOLUTION (1974)
1 Mr. Brown **2** Soul Rebel **3** Try Me **4** It's Alright **5** No Sympathy **6** My Cup **7** Duppy Conqueror **8** Rebel's Hop **9** Cornerstone **10** 400 Years **11** No Water **12** Reaction **13** Soul Almighty **14** Lively Up Yourself **15** Trench Town Rock **16** African Herbsman

LIVE! (1975)
1 Trench Town Rock **2** Burnin' And Lootin' **3** Them Belly Full (But We Hungry) **4** Lively Up Yourself **5** No Woman, No Cry **6** I Shot The Sheriff **7** Get Up, Stand Up

RASTAMAN VIBRATION (1976)

1 Positive Vibration **2** Roots, Rock, Reggae **3** Johnny Was **4** Cry To Me **5** Want More **6** Crazy Baldhead **7** Who The Cap Fit **8** Night Shift **9** War **10** Rat Race **11** Jah Live

"There's a strength and guts to Rastaman Vibration that, almost incredibly, surpasses anything the Wailers and Bob Marley have achieved so far."
SOUNDS ON RASTAMAN VIBRATION

"Marley's imperious as he whiplashes out the command to move ... you'd have to be deaf to resist. So purposeful; it's all delivered with an authority that convinces. Majestic."
SOUNDS ON EXODUS

EXODUS (1977)

1 Natural Mystic **2** So Much Things To Say **3** Guiltiness **4** The Heathen **5** Exodus **6** Jammin' **7** Waiting In Vain **8** Turn Your Lights Down Low **9** Three Little Birds **10** One Love/People Get Ready **11** Jammin' **12** Punky Reggae Party

KAYA (1978)

1 Easy Skanking **2** Kaya **3** Is This Love **4** Sun Is Shining **5** Satisfy My Soul **6** She's Gone **7** Misty Morning **8** Crisis **9** Running Away **10** Time Will Tell **11** Smile Jamaica

BABYLON BY BUS (1978)

1 Positive Vibration **2** Punky Reggae Party **3** Exodus **4** Stir It Up **5** Rat Race **6** Concrete Jungle **7** Kinky Reggae **8** Lively Up Yourself **9** Rebel Music (Three O'Clock Roadblock) **10** Medley: War/No More Trouble **11** Is This Love **12** Heathen **13** Jammin'

"Judging from the title, the mood, the passive nature of the tempo and the fact that the third line on the album is Excuse me while I light my spliff, Id say this album is Marleys Sgt. Pepper."
MELODY MAKER ON KAYA

"Marley continues to expand the boundaries of a music he helped create."
CRAWDADDY ON KAYA

"Survival is akin to a swift kick in the head. Ironically this is his most commercial effort musically."
BILLBOARD ON SURVIVAL

"Redemption Song—such a tour de force, like much of Uprising, is as moving as it is deeply troubling."
ROLLING STONE ON UPRISING

SURVIVAL (1979)

1 So Much Trouble In The World **2** Zimbabwe **3** Top Rankin' **4** Babylon System **5** Survival **6** Africa Unite **7** One Drop **8** Ride Natty Ride **9** Ambush In The Night **10** Wake Up And Live **11** Ride Natty Ride

UPRISING (1980)

1 Coming In From The Cold **2** Real Situation **3** Bad Card **4** We And Dem **5** Work **6** Zion Train **7** Pimper's Paradise **8** Could You Be Loved **9** Forever Loving Jah **10** Redemption Song **11** Redemption Song

"This album seems remarkably true to the general vision of Bob Marley's albums ... any Bob Marley fan ought to own this album."
ALL MUSIC GUIDE ON CONFRONTATION

"What could be a more fitting legacy for Bob Marley? ... a punctuation to a long and unfathomably important career, it serves as an ellipsis."
TROUSER PRESS ON CONFRONTATION

CONFRONTATION (1983)

1 Chant Down Babylon **2** Buffalo Soldier **3** Jump Nyabinghi **4** Mix Up, Mix Up **5** Give Thanks And Praises **6** Blackman Redemption **7** Trench Town **8** Stiff Necked Fools **9** I Know **10** Rastaman Live Up!

LEGEND (1984)

1 Is This Love **2** No Woman, No Cry **3** Could You Be Loved **4** Three Little Birds **5** Buffalo Soldier **6** Get Up, Stand Up **7** Stir It Up **8** Easy Skanking **9** One Love/People Get Ready **10** I Shot The Sheriff **11** Waiting In Vain **12** Redemption Song **13** Satisfy My Soul **14** Exodus **15** Jammin' **16** Punky Reggae Party

4

AWARDS & CHART HISTORY

AUSZEICHNUNGEN & CHARTPLATZIERUNGEN

RÉCOMPENSES ET HISTORIQUE DES VENTES

UNITED STATES CERTIFICATIONS
UNITED STATES ALBUMS
Burnin' – Gold **/ *Songs Of Freedom*** – Double Platinum **/ *Confrontation*** – Gold **/ *Exodus*** – Gold **/ *Kaya*** – Gold **/ *Live!*** – Gold **/ *Rastaman Vibration*** – Gold **/ *Uprising*** – Gold **/ *Natural Mystic*** – Gold **/ *Legend*** – 10 Times Platinum **/ *Chant Down Babylon*** – Gold

UNITED KINGDOM CERTIFICATIONS
UNITED KINGDOM SINGLES
Is This Love – Silver **/** *Jammin'* – Silver **/** *No Woman, No Cry* – Silver **/** *Sun Is Shining* – Silver (Bob Marley vs. Funkstar De Luxe)

UNITED KINGDOM ALBUMS
Live – Silver **/ *Exodus*** – Gold **/ *Kaya*** – Gold **/ *Burnin'*** – Silver **/ *Natty Dread*** – Gold **/ *Catch A Fire*** – Silver **/ *Rastaman Vibration*** – Gold **/ *Songs Of Freedom*** – Silver **/ *Legend*** – 6 Times Platinum **/ *Natural Mystic*** – Gold **/ *One Love: The Very Best Of Bob Marley And The Wailers*** – Gold **/ *Africa Unite: The Singles Collection*** – Gold

AWARDS
Centenary Medal, Council of the Institute of Jamaica – 1970, 1979 **/** Band of the Year, **Rolling Stone** – 1976 **/** Peace Medal of the Third World, United Nations – 1978 **/** Jamaican Order of Merit – 1981 **/** Inducted into the Rock and Roll Hall of Fame – 1994 **/** Album of the Century, **Time *(Exodus)*** – 1999 **/** Star on the Hollywood Walk of Fame – 2001 **/** Grammy Lifetime Achievement Award – 2001 **/** Number 11, 100 Greatest Artists of All Time, **Rolling Stone** – 2004 **/** Inducted into the United Kingdom Hall of Fame – 2004 **/ *Exodus*** inducted into the Grammy Hall of Fame – 2006 **/** 34 Ridgmount Gardens declared a Heritage Site – 2006 **/** Statue unveiled in Serbia – 2008

CHART HISTORY

US CHART SINGLES

Week of Entry	Highest Position	Wks	Title	Catalog Number
73 (July 3, 1976)	51 (July 17, 1976)	6	Roots, Rock, Reggae	Island IS 060

US CHART ALBUMS

Week of Entry	Highest Position	Wks	Title	Catalog Number
190 (May 10, 1975)	92 (September 20, 1975)	27	Natty Dread	Island ILPS 9281
188 (October 11, 1975)	151 (November 1, 1975)	6	Burnin'	Island ILPS 9256
196 (November 8, 1975)	171 (December 6, 1975)	5	Catch A Fire	Island ILPS 9241
40 (May 15, 1976)	8 (July 3, 1976)	22	Rastaman Vibration	Island ILPS 9383
128 (October 23, 1976)	90 (December 4, 1976)	9	Live!	Island ILPS 9376
87 (June 11, 1977)	20 (August 20, 1977)	24	Exodus	Island ILPS 9498
123 (April 22, 1978)	50 (May 27, 1978)	17	Kaya	Island ILPS 9517
130 (December 16, 1978)	102 (February 17, 1979)	16	Babylon By Bus	Island 11
142 (November 17, 1979)	70 (December 15, 1979)	14	Survival	Island ILPS 9542
89 (August 9, 1980)	45 (October 4, 1980)	23	Uprising	Island ILPS 9596
135 (October 31, 1981)	117 (November 28, 1981)	6	Chances Are	Cotillion 5228
148 (July 2, 1983)	55 (August 6, 1983)	15	Confrontation	Island 90085
168 (August 18, 1984)	54 (October 27, 1984)	113	Legend	Island 90169
198 (September 6, 1986)	140 (September 27, 1986)	9	Rebel Music	Island 90520
179 (February 23, 1991)	103 (May 18, 1991)	13	Talkin' Blues	Tuff Gong 848243
87 (October 24, 1992)	86 (October 31, 1992)	15	Songs Of Freedom	Island 12280
67 (June 10, 1995)	67 (June 10, 1995)	14	Natural Mystic	Tuff Gong 24103
79 (December 4, 1999)	60 (January 29, 2000)	24	Chant Down Babylon	Tuff Gong/Island 546404
60 (June 9, 2001)	60 (June 9, 2001)	16	One Love: The Very Best Of Bob Marley And The Wailers	UTV 542855

UK CHART SINGLES

Week of Entry	Highest Position	Wks	Title	Catalog Number
40 (September 27, 1975)	8 (July 18, 1981)	18	No Woman, No Cry	Island WIP 6244
41 (June 25, 1977)	14 (July 30, 1977)	9	Exodus	Island WIP 6390
44 (September 10, 1977)	27 (October 8, 1977)	6	Waiting In Vain	Island WIP 6402
41 (December 10, 1977)	9 (February 4, 1978)	12	Jammin'/Punky Reggae Party	Island WIP 6410
35 (February 25, 1978)	9 (April 1, 1978)	9	Is This Love	Island WIP 6420
52 (June 10, 1978)	21 (July 22, 1978)	10	Satisfy My Soul	Island WIP 6440
62 (October 20, 1979)	56 (November 3, 1979)	4	So Much Trouble In The World	Island WIP 6510
46 (June 21, 1980)	5 (July 19, 1980)	12	Could You Be Loved	Island WIP 6610
73 (September 13, 1980)	17 (October 4, 1980)	9	Three Little Birds	Tuff Gong/Island WIP 6641
56 (May 7, 1983)	4 (June 11, 1983)	12	Buffalo Soldier	Tuff Gong/Island IS 108
35 (April 21, 1984)	5 (May 19, 1984)	11	One Love/People Get Ready (Medley)	Island IS 169
41 (June 23, 1984)	31 (July 7, 1984)	7	Waiting In Vain	Island IS 180
72 (December 8, 1984)	71 (December 15, 1984)	2	Could You Be Loved	Island IS 210
45 (May 18, 1991)	42 (May 25, 1991)	3	One Love/People Get Ready (Medley)	Tuff Gong TGX 1
11 (September 19, 1992)	5 (October 3, 1992)	9	Iron Lion Zion	Tuff Gong TGXCD 2
42 (November 28, 1992)	42 (November 28, 1992)	4	Why Should I/Exodus	Tuff Gong TGXCD 3
17 (May 20, 1995)	17 (May 20, 1995)	4	Keep On Moving	Tuff Gong TGXCD 4

Week of Entry	Highest Position	Wks	Title	Catalog Number
42 (June 8, 1996)	42 (June 8, 1996)	1	**What Goes Around Comes Around**	Anansi ANACS 002
3 (September 25, 1999)	3 (September 25, 1999)	10	**Sun Is Shining***	Club Tools/Edel 0066895
15 (December 11, 1999)	15 (December 11, 1999)	7	**Turn Your Lights Down Low****	Columbia 6684362
11 (January 22, 2000)	11 (January 22, 2000)	6	**Rainbow Country***	Club Tools CLU 0067225
42 (June 24, 2000)	42 (June 24, 2000)	2	**Jammin'***	Tuff Gong TGXCD 9
58 (November 12, 2005)	58 (November 12, 2005)	1	**No Woman, No Cry**	Tuff Gong TGXCD13
67 (November 19, 2005)	67 (November 19, 2005)	1	**I Shot The Sheriff**	Tuff Gong TGXCD14
54 (November 26, 2005)	54 (November 26, 2005)	1	**Sun Is Shining**	Tuff Gong TGXCD15
45 (December 3, 2005)	45 (December 3, 2005)	1	**Slogans**	Tuff Gong TGXCDS11
49 (December 10, 2005)	49 (December 10, 2005)	1	**Africa Unite**	Tuff Gong TGXCD16
56 (December 17, 2005)	56 (December 17, 2005)	1	**Stand Up Jamrock**	Tuff Gong TGXCD17

UK CHART ALBUMS

Week of Entry	Highest Position	Wks	Title	Catalog Number
47 (October 4, 1975)	43 (November 1, 1975)	5	**Natty Dread**	Island ILPS 9281
44 (December 20, 1975)	38 (December 27, 1975)	11	**Live!**	Island ILPS 9376
30 (May 8, 1976)	15 (May 15, 1976)	13	**Rastaman Vibration**	Island ILPS 9383
22 (June 11, 1977)	8 (July 2, 1977)	55	**Exodus**	Island ILPS 9498
19 (April 1, 1978)	4 (April 8, 1978)	24	**Kaya**	Island ILPS 9517
40 (December 16, 1978)	40 (December 16, 1978)	11	**Babylon By Bus**	Island ISLD 11
34 (October 13, 1979)	20 (October 20, 1979)	6	**Survival**	Island ILPS 9542
14 (June 28, 1980)	6 (July 12, 1980)	17	**Uprising**	Island ILPS 9596
8 (May 28, 1983)	5 (June 4, 1983)	19	**Confrontation**	Island ILPS 9760
1 (May 19, 1984)	1 (May 19, 1984)	339	**Legend**	Tuff Gong BMWCD 1
54 (June 28, 1986)	54 (June 28, 1986)	3	**Rebel Music**	Island ILPS 9843
10 (October 3, 1992)	10 (October 3, 1992)	5	**Songs Of Freedom**	Tuff Gong TGCBX 1
5 (June 3, 1995)	5 (June 3, 1995)	8	**Natural Mystic**	Tuff Gong BMWCD 2
56 (September 4, 1999)	40 (September 11, 1999)	3	**Sun Is Shining***	Club Tools CLU 66730
5 (June 2, 2001)	5 (June 2, 2001)	15	**One Love: The Very Best Of Bob Marley And The Wailers**	Tuff Gong BMWCD 3
75 (July 7, 2001)	75 (July 7, 2001)	1	**Lively Up Yourself**	Music Collection 12691
24 (November 10, 2001)	24 (November 10, 2001)	8	**One Love: The Very Best Of Bob Marley And The Wailers**	Tuff Gong 5865512
51 (June 5, 2004)	51 (June 5, 2004)	2	**Roots Of A Legend**	Trojan TJODX 176
26 (November 19, 2005)	26 (November 19, 2005)	5	**Africa Unite: The Singles Collection**	Tuff Gong BMWCDX 4

*Bob Marley vs. Funkstar De Luxe
**Bob Marley featuring Lauryn Hill
***Bob Marley featuring MC Lyte

BIBLIOGRAPHY

Crampton, Luke & Dafydd Rees: *Rock & Roll. Year By Year.* Dorling Kindersley, 2003.
Farley, Christopher John: *Before The Legend. The Rise Of Bob Marley.* Amistad, 2006.
Henke, James: *Marley Legend.* Chronicle, 2006.
Jaffe, Lee: *One Love. Life With Bob Marley & The Wailers.* W. W. Norton, 2003.
Lazell, Barry: *Marley. The Illustrated Legend.* Hamlyn, 1994.

Marley, Rita: *No Woman, No Cry. My Life With Bob Marley.* Hyperion, 2004.
Paprocki, Sherry Beck: *Bob Marley.* Chelsea House, 2006.
Steffens, Roger & Leroy Jodie Pierson: *The DefinitiveDiscography.* Rounder, 2005.
White, Timothy: *Catch A Fire. The Life Of Bob Marley.* Henry Holt, 1983.
Williams, Richard: *Exodus. Exile 1977.* Weidenfeld & Nicolson, 2007.

IMPRINT

© 2009 TASCHEN GmbH
Hohenzollernring 53, D-50672 Köln
www.taschen.com

Editor: Luke Crampton & Dafydd Rees/
Original Media/www.orginal-media.net
Picture Research: Dafydd Rees & Wellesley Marsh
Editorial Coordination:
Florian Kobler and Mischa Gayring, Cologne
Production Coordination:
Nadia Najm and Horst Neuzner, Cologne
Design: Sense/Net, Andy Disl and Birgit Eichwede, Cologne
German Translation: Anke Burger, Berlin
French Translation: Alice Pétillot, Paris
Multilingual Production: www.arnaudbriand.com, Paris

Printed in Italy
ISBN 978-3-8365-1128-5

To stay informed about upcoming TASCHEN titles, please request our magazine at www.taschen.com/magazine or write to TASCHEN, Hohenzollernring 53, D-50672 Cologne, Germany; contact@taschen.com; Fax: +49-221-254919. We will be happy to send you a free copy of our magazine, which is filled with information about all of our books.

ACKNOWLEDGMENTS

Ralf Gärtner, Arthur Gorson, Meri Hartford, Richard Horsey, Bob Korn, Jörg Krings, Joe Medina, Michelle Press, Sheree Rhoden, Silke Maria Schmidt, Joelle Sedlmeyer, Roger Steffens, Nancy Treves, Chris Wilson, Jon Wilton.

COPYRIGHT